Psychology as King of the Ghosts: A Personal Critique

by

James Russell

KFS

NEWTON-LE-WILLOWS

Published in the United Kingdom in 2018
by The Knives Forks And Spoons Press,
51 Pipit Avenue,
Newton-le-Willows,
Merseyside,
WA12 9RG.

ISBN 978-1-912211-11-1

Cover design by James Crossland-Mills (www.think-jcm.com)

Supported using public funding by

ARTS COUNCIL ENGLAND

LOTTERY FUNDED

Table of Contents

For The Grand-Girls, Leila and Elsa

.

Part One:

King-of-the-Ghosts Psychology

King-of-the-ghosts Psychology

This book has both a dark and a light —lightish — purpose. On the dark side I argue that psychology, not always but often, over-reaches and oversells. It can be fatally wrongheaded about mentality, and seems, on this face, to be the natural habitat of the fraud. Not all psychology, just king-of-the-ghosts psychology — a concept impossible to define crisply. I will say what I mean by king-of-the-ghosts in this first part. The lighter side is autobiographical. This material is not a laugh-a-minute, but it is unbuttoned. Why these two? Because I illustrate in the personal sections how I have been seduced by the ghost-side.

Why should I in particular — indeed, of all people —write a memoir, albeit one more intellectual than personal? I have not lead an interesting life, I am not one of the Big Figures in psychology — and I have never had a breakdown.[1] One answer is that because, after nearly 50 years of doing it, I have some things to say about the nature of psychology. Not only then an *apologia pro vita sua,* but a warning about how psychology has within it the I-suspect-unique potential to go to the bad.

---

[1] One of the inspirations for this book, in its blend of the personal and the psychological, was Stuart Sutherland's book *Breakdown.*

A warning? Over the past 50 years psychology has blossomed, becoming more rigorous, more various, and more closely integrated with other disciples, such as physiology, philosophy and computer science. There would seem to be little point in simply cheering on this process. I do, however, see quite a lot of a point in showing how psychology can go wrong and has gone wrong; though this is not a matter of simply pointing the finger at something meretricious. It's more to do with trying to break the grip of an illusion or, more luridly, it's ghost-busting. To this kind of psychology I bid not farewell, but good riddance.

As I said, there is a more immediate reason why I am doing this in an autobiographical style rather than a dispassionately third-person one. It is that the tendency to think about psychology in the wrong way — in a king-of-the-ghosts way — *has been present in me* from the moment I first heard the word "psychology," and it has taken most of my career to realise this and accommodate to it. It will be clear from the autobiographical section that few people are less naturally hard-headed and scientific than am I. My career has absolutely not been a long battle against the powers of unscientific darkness. For this reason, not because I have any special powers of empathy, I can appreciate why people, from novice undergraduates to venerable researchers, think the way they do; and go wrong the way they do. I have felt the pull in that direction.

This then is the king-of-the-ghosts of the title (a full explanation follows shortly). I have to admit that my target is not a very clear one. Indeed, in this first section of the book it will be characterised in a metaphor-heavy way. Then in the long autobiographical section it will be rendered concrete and names will be named (or not very carefully concealed). It will seep into the narrative, whilst still being presented impressionistically and personally. I should say too that most of the narrative landscape will be peopled by flesh-and-blood psychology, with the ghost making only intermittent appearances; then filling the screen at the end. I think the ghost is best appreciated in the full context of flesh-and-blood psychology. Then in the final section of the book — 'Question Time' — everything will be rendered explicit and defended as best I can.

My position is that there is only one kind of psychology worth bothering with and that is the psychology of *How do we do it?* More precisely, this is the study of our capacities and of the mechanisms that underlie them. This set of capacities enables us to perceive the world, inhibit impulsive reactions to it, plan, feel appropriate emotions, reason; and the rest of it. All this exists against a background of dispositions (e.g., being disposed to aggression). Putting these two together, humans can act freely. Indeed, the idea of our having "free will" seems a perfectly coherent idea to me. Psychology, in short, explains human freedom. It shows how it is empirically possible.[2] The sort of existentialism-lite that this implies will be examined in the final part.

What about the other kind of psychology? The king-of the-ghosts kind? This is human psychology regarded as the study

---

[2] As contrasted with the Kantian project of saying how something is philosophically (or "transcendentally") possible.

of *what we are sometimes like and tend to do*. It collects information about what we tend do and tend to feel. Are we sometimes over-compliant? Do we tend to feel happier after talking to strangers? Do we attribute beliefs to others on thin evidence? Do we lie to ourselves about what our preferences really are? On this kind of psychology there is something — The Mind — that is not a set of capacities, but is an entity that has an essential character to be studied in terms of what we tend to do.

Thus far, it just looks as if I have it in for social psychology. Not really; and anyway my target lies deeper than that. For I shall be arguing that the notion of The Mind as an object of study is an incoherent notion, because there are only *minds*, and minds are points-of-view — individuals' views from somewheres. There cannot be a view from everywhere. More immediately, it seems to me that practitioners of these what-we-tend-to-do studies, which may in fact be no more than a kind of statistical journalism, elevate their enterprise by saying their topic is "the mind." People do this and this and this *because the human mind is such-and-such.*

You may, by now, have come to the view that this will be a sour book by somebody tired of psychology after nearly half a century of doing it. Not so. My enthusiasm for psychology — for the un-ghostly kind — is undiminished after all this time. Yes, I have sat through seminars and lectures on the ghost-psychology wiping away tears of boredom,[3] I have failed to understand more talks on low-level vision and fine-grain

---

[3]   This phrase was stolen from James Fenton.

neuroscience than I have had hot dinners, but nearly every time I go to one of our departmental seminars I come away with something, something to think about, and feeling that things are moving forward. The scope for this kind of psychology would seem to be infinite. And it would indeed be so, were it not for one thing: the mind-body problem. By this I mean that to every sane mind two kinds of existence present themselves: a refractory physical world, and a mental world of how-it-is-with me. How are these (causally?) related? What neuroimaging delivers is something that's more like rubbing-our-noses-in-the-problem than a route to dissolving it.

Does all this imply that there will be a lot of laying-down-the-law? Some. And yet I hope my gaudy title will move us away from stern-faced taxonomising towards something more subjective and personal. So, now to explain the title properly.

Why *ghost*? Along with "quantum leap," "learning curve," and a few others "The Ghost in the Machine" is one of those sciencey/philosophical phrases that have entered everyday discourse. Probably, Arthur Koestler's book of that title did more to aid the process than did its coiner — Gilbert Ryle in his *The Concept of Mind*. Ryle used this expression to describe his target: the view, associated with Descartes, that the mental is something over-and-above all the various cognitive functions and mechanisms, a *sui generis* free-floating something-or-other. To think that it is such an entity is to have fallen victim to the kind of "category mistake" not unique to this domain. Accordingly, in Ryle's example, a visitor to a university town is shown around the university — the lecture halls and labs, the residencies and offices — after which he asks: "But where is the *university?*" As if there were a central something of which these were mere adjuncts.

It is clear that Ryle's point lands in the same ball-park as the kind of worry about psychology I've just been expressing. Yet this does absolutely not mean that I'm any kind of Rylean — any kind of "logical behaviourist." Nobody desires less to hark back to Behaviourism and, indeed, to the indefensible view that all talk of mental life as being a *sui generis* something is a glaring category mistake. I am thinking here of my philosophy tutor Harold Cox casually defusing Ryle's view that "enjoying X" should be cashed out in terms of certain overt behaviours (e.g., not wanting to be interrupted), leaving no phenomenal residue, no "ghost" at all. My position is light years from that; indeed it will emerge in the final part that I am a (harmless) kind of dualist. But Ryle *was* onto something. He was right to say that, when we come to the science of psychology, we delude ourselves in thinking that there is a category "the mental," set apart from vision, hearing, reasoning, memory, emotion, and so forth, about which we can have objective knowledge of the kind we can have about the physical world. None of this is to deny, by the way, that each of us has a sense of self — of a focal point and prime mover of our of mental lives set apart from seeing, reasoning, etc. The denial is about psychology as a discipline not about individual mentalities. I will return to this. Now to complete the explanation of the gaudy chapter title.

Why *King of?* Because those I diagnose as believing they are experts on The Mind, based on science-lite studies of what we tend to do and feel, are regally positing a ghostly discipline containing a repository of information on how it is with the subjects — with the workers and the drones. They suffer from ego-inflation. My motivation for using "ghost" here is partly rhetorical, springing from a desire to soften and lighten the tone of what I will be saying. As I said before, I do not wish to taxonomise and lay down the law about who should study what and how. The idea is to say how it strikes me and to sound a warning. And for help in articulating how it strikes me I turned to a poem by Wallace Stevens called *A Rabbit as King of the Ghosts*. The poem is written as if the rabbit were speaking at the end of the day in late summer. There is reference to a cat "slopping" its milk, then to the cat being "forgotten on the moon." And then the tercet:

And to feel that the light is a rabbit-light
In which everything is meant for you
And nothing needs to be explained;

Then later:

The grass is full

And full of yourself. The trees around are for you,
The whole of the wilderness of night is for you,
A self that touches all edges,

You become a self that fills the four corners of night.
The red cat hides away in fur-light.

I have no wish to "resolve" the poem, nor would I claim to know exactly what Stevens had in mind.

For my purposes the egocentrism or ego-inflation of the rabbit conjures up a possible state of the individual mind, as described by psychologists like Piaget: the confusion between the world as it is *manifest to me from here* and the idea that how it appears to me *exhausts all that can be said about reality*. The trap into which we, as well as what another poet called "Piaget's babies,"[4] can fall is the idea that our own mind is the regnant mind — and that's it. The regnant mind can re-colour a cat (from red to green) and see it as a mere bug. And finally it becomes as solid and fixed as a statue in its false belief ("like a carving in space"). And as I write this I come to think that maybe what Stevens had in mind was the mental hubris of mankind after the "death" of God.

We have then, two things: the rabbit's false belief that he's mentally king-of-the-world (paralleling the hubris of some psychology), and the true belief that there is no one mind, but a plethora of rabbit-minds. The false idea is king-of the ghosts-psychology. Why bother with the poem at all? Why not have cooler terms? It's all a matter of tone. If there has to be any kind of taxonomy then I want it to be a relaxed, impressionistic, and defeasible one written out of one rabbit-mind.

To call this a "subjective" book is not a sly way of evading the possibility that what I am saying may be contradictory, conceptually empty, or empirically wrong. It's all very well hedging that: "Anyway this is how it seems to me." Because, somebody is perfectly entitled to reply: "Well that is not how it

---

[4]   This is William Empson in his poem "Your Teeth are Ivory Towers."

should seem to you. And if you applied your intelligence properly it would not do so!" When I have done with the autobiographising I will return to these themes more formally and deal with objections.

There are a number of reasons for including an autobiographical section, and the central one is to illustrate how somebody can begin with firm faith in the existence of king-of the-ghosts-psychology, believing that there is a body of knowledge out there about "what makes us tick," and then to come to the view, rather late in my case, that human psychology is the study of competences/capacities, not of mental essence. I'm sure this is not the *usual* "trajectory" (as we developmentalists call it). A colleague of mine (ex-Oxford, now Harvard), of my generation and, like me, from an arts background said that he came to psychology because it was wide open, because its — this was not his way of putting it — scientifically un-developed state meant that it was relatively easy to be original. He has certainly made a bigger mark than I have. And I would bet good money that there is a host of people out there in their late teens whose view of psychology is just like my "starting-state" (again, as developmentalists call it). This view is a deeply contradictory one: psychology is like science insofar as it is a body of objective knowledge, but at the same time it is quite unlike science insofar as it is about the warm, welcoming world of people, where there is room for debate in a way there's not in the mainstream sciences. It is as human as you could wish and it affords wisdom about the ways of everybody from the man in the corner shop to Madam

Bovary. You think it's *interesting*, and everybody agrees with you.

A further reason for including the autobiographical section is that it will, I hope, show how we got to here from 1966. Psychology is fashion-driven, and chronicling the shifts and strata of fashion over the past 50 years should provide a good basis on which to re-consider, re-express, and defend the ideas I have just sketched in.

My initial motivation for writing this book was a purely polemical one. I had come to feel that psychology was becoming a Wizard of Oz, and that it was time to pull back the curtain and reveal the old humbug who can deliver no more than placebo-trinkets — a diploma, a medal, and a pocket watch. The author as Toto. Of course, this is too extreme. It is easy to fall into that way of thinking. How often do we hear the following of kind of thing: "a psychologist" tells us whether a celebrity paedophile is or is not evil, or whether in choosing a female trainer Andy Murray is revealing a degree of mother-fixation, or tells us on the *Today* Programme that Muslim school-girls who wear the hijab have higher (or maybe lower) "self worth" than those who do not? And then, more dangerously, I would consider degrees in psychology. Do we actually *know* enough to fill three years of psychology teaching? Think of all those people in the UK who have First Class degrees in psychology. Are these degrees in any sense the equivalent of Firsts in modern languages or chemistry? They are tests of intelligence insofar as they are tests of memory, writing ability, applied common sense and maths; but what has been memorised? The pros and cons of a lot of defunct or silly theories, a mosaic of experimental studies that are all in their different ways problematic (a narrative of failed attempts to nail something down), how to use statistical packages to run correlations and tests of significance; and how to dress up approximate, provisional knowledge as if it were science? And to witness the banality of the popular psychology books — the ones written by professors in good universities, I mean, not by Paul McKenna figures — books that explain how experimental psychology has revealed to us that the self is an illusion, that explain the nature of evil in terms of lack of a functioning "empathy circuit."

This is just blanket negativity. Why should psychologists not have their say? Also, there are some wonderful psychology degrees around and brilliant young people getting them. Popular books can contain wrongheadedness and yet, nonetheless, inspire talented people to dig deeper by taking a university degree. And yet the scepticism about psychology remains. It is eradicable. It is so in me, at least. What seems to ground the scepticism is that psychology will always deliver less than it promises to deliver as long as people are operating on the king-of-the-ghosts side of things. I aim to show how a career in psychology can lead to this view: not so much tearing down a humbug's curtain as ending up with the refrain: "Search for the humbug inside yourself."

Now for some consumer warnings. This is not a *researched* book, by which I mean that I will make all kinds of generalisations about psychology which could have been backed up or nuanced after a spot of judicious Googling; but have not been. As I said, my approach is subjective and impressionistic. These generalisations will often be anodyne and difficult to deny (e.g., *of course* psychology degrees have mushroomed since the '60s, and *of course* psycho-types are all over the media nowadays).

The next consumer warning is about the naming of names. When what I have to say about somebody is neutral or positive or part of an anecdote I will use the person's name. When I am using the individual to make a negative point I will give as little information about them as possible, invent a name for them, and asterisk the *first* mention — such as Dr. Fabian Klein* and Jonquil Haitch.* Similarly for ideas and their acronyms : Phenomenological Analytical Hermeneutical Research Trajectory* (or P.H.A.R.T.*) and for books: *Reasons Why "You" Don't Actually Exist.**

Why do I do this? Mainly because these pseudonyms are supposed to describe types of people, books, and theories encountered in psychology. They do not merely target particular referents.

And finally to the matter of what I earlier called "tone." Despite the subjectivity of the treatment, I will not be telling the reader about my first racing bike and how I felt when the *The Journal of Experimental Child Psychology* rejected my first paper. It will be intellectually subjective, not personally subjective — except here and there when the personal and the professional blend. And the tone will sometimes have more in common with Adrian Mole than with *The Prelude,* with the protagonist being more of a *Zelig* than the autobiographical Bertrand Russell.

And now for a caveat-cum-spoiler. In the subsequent narrative, king-of-the-ghosts psychology will mainly appear in the early and late stages — in my years as an undergraduate in Oxford and then as a senior academic at Cambridge. From 1968 to 2012 the ghost will be almost entirely a phenomenon within this author; though the fact that it reappeared shows it was there all the time working towards a DSc from Ghost College. It will manifest itself in a number of ways, mainly as a tendency to be captured by a vision of what humans are like essentially, a vision borrowed from some charismatic theorist perhaps. This is bad because it generates a kind of ego-inflated superiority to the spadework of experimental psychology and leads one to launch research programs buoyed up only by one's own intellectual crushes. I have to admit though — I hope this will emerge — that a *homeopathic* dose of it gets you going, and may indeed get you running experiments. If these experiments fail (as they probably will) then that's no bad thing. I'm reminded of here of a routine by an American comic, whose name I never caught. Referring to these signs you see in the backs of cars like "Back off, baby on board" he said: "When I see them I always overtake then brake hard. Bounce the kid around a bit. Give it a sense of *realidy.*" Quite! A good point, and also a rather Piagetian one.[5] The external world of data is a refractory place.

---

[5] The world as a refractory entity to which the child has to "accommodate" looms large in Piagetian theory.

Part Two:

Let's Make a Career of it

In the stage of concrete operations[6]

Setting aside the possibility that I might have seen, on returning from Sunday School one day, Donald Broadbent[7] on the Brains Trust, my first experience of or brush with psychology arose through my hatred of school. To explain: if you cannot do arithmetic and live in fear of it, if you have a stammer that makes reading aloud in class a torment, and if your headmaster, while having the appearance of a Sir Bufton Tufton,[8] has the temperament of a cliquish, spiteful child, then you will tend to do anything in your power to avoid school. What was in my power was acting ill. My speciality was acute stomach pains, with migraines coming late to the feast. It did require some memorial skill — recalling the nature and locus of the pains — as well as the ability to bind (as cognitive psychologists say) nature of pain to locus.

---

[6] This is the developmental stage between about 7 and about 12 in Jean Piaget's developmental theory.

[7] Donald Broadbent was a psychologist of huge impact. His interest in selective attention in the 1960s was one of the factors that released us from the grip of behaviourism.

[8] This is *Private Eye's* canonical Tory back-bencher.

Be that as it may, my acting was so good that I ended up in hospital "under observation." I never gave a second's thought to the anxiety I was causing my parents as long as I was escaping Victoria Park Juniors. This was in South Bristol by the way.

It cannot have been difficult to spot the fraud, as I would usually begin the day with pain contortions, then drift up to see my dad in his workshop — he was an upholsterer — after a hearty lunch. The NHS had the resources to play safe in those days. Of course, the Bristol Royal Infirmary found, after various tests, nothing; and so I was discharged and my case passed to a man who must have been an educational or clinical psychologist. Some weeks after my discharge my mother took me to see this person, who spoke to us separately. I knew the game was up and told him about my hatred of school, venturing the theory that this had brought on stomach cramps. I didn't mention the arithmetic and the reading aloud and instead shared my thoughts on a shouty master of a lower form, and my shame (shame invented, though not the incident) at being caught red-handed, as a tuck-shop server, with a fistful of chocolate biscuits and no money in the till. He was a benign person, but you did not have to be Ronnie Laing[9] to work out that he knew that I knew that he knew that I knew that he was onto me.

While one can be breezy about this long after the event, for me it was more Dostoyevsky than Richmal Crompton. The Eleven Plus was looming, the examination that, in those days,

---

[9] The radical psychiatrist R. D. Laing wrote a book I shall touch on later in which he described social thought-embedding of this kind.

decided children's educational, and therefore social fate. At this point psychology pops up again. Why have the decisive and divisive examination at 11 years of age? Apparently, educational psychologists believed then — principal among them "The Old Delinquent"[10] Sir Cyril Burt — that one's IQ does not change after eleven.

With regard to my more direct encounter with educational psychology, I have to admit that it did not encourage me to wonder about what psychology might be. I didn't care. In recent years we have made giant strides, thanks to the work of Sarah-Jayne Blakemore[11] among others, in our understanding of the neurocognitive changes that take place during adolescence (though Piagetian theory is important here too). The sometimes-morbid self-consciousness of the adolescent could be seen as a symptom of a deeper appreciation of the individual mental life that exists "behind" social life: others can see what I am mentally up to just by looking. I suppose what I thought about psychology and psychologists was something along the lines that you had better watch out because they can see what you're really up to mentally. I continued to invent illnesses to escape school duties, while abandoning the pain-drama.

---

[10] Sir Cyril Burt wrote a book called "The Young Delinquent." His data on the heritability of IQ have been shown to have been fraudulent; though intelligence is certainly heritable to some degree.

[11] A good book on this: S-J. Blakemore and U. Frith *The Learning Brain* (New Jersey: Wiley-Blackwell, 2005).
(Blackwell)

Informal operations[12]

I managed to get through only two of the four-or-five pages of arithmetic questions on the Eleven Plus. I scraped a pass, nonetheless, and was lucky enough to be placed in the B (grammar, just) stream of a new comprehensive. This time the headmaster was charismatic and eccentric. When I encountered Proust's Baron de Charlus in later years it evoked an image of John Dicker with his fur collar and cigarette holder. He was so extravert a stutterer that he didn't realise he actually had one, admonishing me thus: "I c-conquered my st-stutter Jim-Jim-Jimmy by simply articulating into a m-mirror."

While I was "neurocognitively" ripe to think about psychology I had to wait a number of years for the "environmental trigger." I can't pretend to know much about these triggers. Certainly some biology and German lessons spring to mind. Word got around that our biology teacher Mr Shepherd —we called him "Hancock" as he looked like a bohemian Tony Hancock— had taken some undergraduate courses in psychology. In my recollection it was mainly the

---

[12] This is a reference to the "formal operations" of which Piaget claimed the adolescent to be capable.

girls who begged, if a lesson finished early, "please can you tell us about psychology Sir." He explained the difference between a child pantomiming being a steam train and a schizophrenic doing the same thing by saying that the child can just drop it and come in for his tea, whereas the schizophrenic will say that he would "scratch his paintwork" squeezing in through the front door.

The truly memorable event for me was one of our German masters (Bob Summers) making the throwaway remark that Kafka's famous short story Metamorphosis, in which a boy wakes up as a beetle, had been thought to refer to schizophrenia. Now you're talking! Bob Summers also said that Goethe's IQ had been estimated at 165. This had much less of an impact because when you are falling for king-of-the-ghosts psychology schizophrenia really is your Number One. Why? because it promises a kind of pop-up-book illustration of what-people-can-be-like. Because, for somebody beginning to be interested in psychology the schizophrenic presents a lurid cartoon of a possible mental life. Pascal said that "small minds are concerned with the extraordinary, great minds with the ordinary." If "small" means "unformed" and "great" means "mature" then this fits the present case (I need hardly add that this is not intended to insult schizophrenia researchers!).

It was not so much schizophrenia in itself that did it for me as the combination of literature and a compelling psychological category. I will come back to the question of why madness in general and schizophrenia in particular attracts certain would-be psychologists. In any event, lessons also stimulated psychological interest of a more sober kind. One day in a Latin lesson I wondered how it was that Roman children two thousand years ago were able to learn all this stuff so easily, while we were sweating over it. Were they different from us, I wondered? If somebody had told me about Chomsky's demolition of the Skinnerian view of first-language learning[13] and about the revolution it sparked in cognitive psychology I doubt that I would have been interested. After all, what had that got to do with....*The Mind*!

I really don't know why, but the category of the psychological was formed, within this adolescent mind — from literature, not from science. To associate the world of Hook's Law, semi-permeable membranes, things that go pop in a test-tube with The World of The Mind was to make a Rylean category mistake, for me. My case is far from unusual.

Why psychology within literature? Despite not taking English A-Level — here I must shamefully admit that the large amount of reading-round-the-class put me off — I became a reader of novels and an avid listener to The Critics on Radio 3 (Cyril Connolly, Harold Hobson, V. S. Pritchett, Edward Lucie-Smith, Marghanita Laski, Bryan Robertson, George Melly; now that's what I call strength in depth). I shunned the novels my father read (Dickens for example), and having readied myself with Jane Austen, steered towards the heavyweights. "Heavyweight," for me, meant being freighted with something between the philosophy and psychology of human nature. Of course I enjoyed reading Dostoyevsky, Sartre, Becket, Joyce, and — above all — Kafka; but I read them for lessons on

---

[13] In his review of Skinner's book *Verbal Behaviour* Chomsky lampooned the idea that children learn grammar by being reinforced for saying the right things.

human nature (the "art" side of things I left to poetry and painting — attempting both with some success in the latter, and none at all in the former).

The radical pragmatist philosopher Richard Rorty refers to "the phallocentic metaphor of depth."[14] And I suppose this was the metaphor I lived by (if this sounds grim, I should say it was backgrounded by The Rolling Stones). While there is a kind of post-Freudian psychology called Depth Psychology, for me psychology just *was* depth — the plumbing of the depths of human mental life. The idea that it could be done in any way other than through literature and the kind of unbuttoned philosophy that was almost a kind of literature simply did not occur to me. Surely Freud must have come into play? Not really. I read some Freud whilst finding the approach too reductive and the interpretations of the famous case studies florid and implausible. There was also the question of the analyst's *authority*. It lacked mystery too. I suspect my view of The Mind (a king-of-the-ghosts or nothing) was something like the Kantian Noumenon: not "things as they are in themselves," but the mental as it is in itself. The very idea that this could be approached in any other way than via the literary I would have thought philistine.

Let me say, in passing, that how I used to think about psychology before I actually did any cannot be *in itself* of the slightest interest to anybody. I was, however, surely not unique. There's a lot of it about. What's more, this image of The Mind is not only one enjoyed by 6th Form ignoramuses: it

---

14   In an article in the *London Review of Books* on March 16th 2000.

is the default image that you tend to have unless you view human psychology as the study of human competence. That is my contention and diagnosis.

Before going to university I had one further brush with educational psychology. My speech therapist — this in a bad patch of stammering — put me in touch with a colleague of hers who was an educational psychologist. I nearly abandoned my psychology ambition because of it. Up I went to this man's fine house in Clifton. He explained to me that psychology was a science and showed me the books with pictures of brains and — God help us — *graphs* in them. "Yes," I said with a sigh, "I suppose it must be a science." His demeanour didn't help. He was a cold fish who ended his utterances (nicely balancing my stutterances) with a forced smile that was immediately switched off like a light. I asked whether a psychologist should have a certain kind of personality. "Well, a certain degree of *warmth* is required, one might say" [grin—off].

I chose for my School Prize for Latin (not much competition) Ernst Breisach's *Introduction to Modern Existentialism*. I could take or leave Paul Tillich and one or two others. Kierkegaard and Sartre were the boys for me. I thought it was a wonderful book and read every word at least once. I mention this because I shall return to existentialism in the final section when I say that much I what I will have said by that time is consistent with a kind of existentialism. Like no other animal, human beings are free, in a special sense. What we know about the neuroscience of intentional action, the genes' role in temperament, and the effects of early rearing on later development and so forth does not contradict this view: it makes it all the more plausible. Scientific psychology shows us how this freedom is possible, rather than eroding our belief in it. If you take this view, there *can* be no king-of-the-ghosts psychology.

A huge amount of money must have changed hands in the staffroom on the day I heard I had been accepted into Oxford to read Psychology and Philosophy (PPP). I was a notoriously lazy, unfocussed backslider and frequent-clown; and the only 6th Former never to be made a prefect. I had a year in hand before I went up, which I *irritatingly* used to burnish a philo-psych persona garnished with free (of course) jazz listening, with Vorticist-like paint-daubing, and with a crew-cut and a green mohair suit. I was such a jazzy snob I turned down the chance of seeing Dylan at The Colston Hall in his Blonde-on-Blonde glory. Riding for a fall?

The Wide-Awake Spires

Animal behaviour and logic

My educational psychologist with the punctuating smile was correct. No, there were no lectures on how Kafka's *The Castle* illustrates the essential goal-directed futility of human life, nor on the question of why Joyce refers to the "ineluctable modality of the visible." There was, though, a lot about herring-gull chicks, formal logic, and whether "exists" is a predicate. In those days — and nowadays too for all I know — in PPP[15] the student began with animal behaviour for psychology and formal and informal logic for philosophy. Then a Prelim exam, the failing of which is not recommended.

I assumed that The Mind would come along later. Meanwhile, if you are going to study ethology then you can't do much better than have Niko Tinbergen as one of your lecturers and Richard Dawkins as another. Tinbergen was elegant in a 1940s-style suit, and dryly witty. Somebody got the time wrong and turned up about an hour late: "I hope you don't

---

[15] Psychology, Philosophy, and Physiology. The undergraduate takes only one of the latter two and must take the first. I believe there is now Psychology, Philosophy, and Linguistics, that works in much the same way.

mind. We started without you." Dawkins was boyish and amused, saying at one point — I have no idea why this has proved so memorable — "When a stickleback feels *sexy*." I read about Tinbergen's drive-based theory of animal social behaviour (rather Freudian), and it was pretty obvious even to me that this was recognisable a kind of psychology — though without The Mind of course.

I was lucky in two respects. First, the Experimental Psychology Fellow in Lincoln College was N. J. (Nick) Mackintosh; and my tutorial partner (though he was at Trinity, not Lincoln) was Keith Stenning. Nick was a brilliant teacher. Nothing flashy, just all the necessary qualities in abundance: extreme lucidity, patience, formidable content knowledge, dry wit, and modesty. With regard to the last two, despite the fact he had a long index-card file of relevant studies and a head full of them, he insisted that as a learning theorist (one who studies the mechanisms of learning in laboratory animals) he was really no expert on animals in their natural environment and so some of the tutoring would have to be done by his wife (a zoologist): "I'm not sure who will be seeing you next week, but if I lose the argument with my wife, it will be me."

In the second place, I was lucky to have Keith as a tutorial partner because, despite being chalk-and-cheese as personalities, we hit it off, and remained friends through Oxford and beyond. In a way, though, I was unlucky in Keith too. Not only towering over me physically — and I am six foot — he towered over me intellectually. What's more, he had a quicksilver mind and had taken Zoology A-level, and so he knew much of the material already — even the stuff on phototaxis (orienting to light stimuli in wormy creatures). Not great for the intellectual self-esteem.

Even in the Oxford science departments in those days undergraduates read out their tutorial essays. Keith went first with an essay on Tinbergen's drive theory ("displacement activity" and so forth — the pressure cooker metaphor) with some clever human analogies. I went second with an essay on "instinct." While Ethologists are no more likely to use that term these days than *elan vital,* it was still a live issue in the late '60s as to whether or not it was useful to refer to animal behaviour as instinctual. Anyway, with the help of a little paperback collection called *Instinct* and quite a few other sources I assembled my essay. Here the difference between the arts-humanities ways of doing things and the science one came into embarrassing relief. John Dicker, in teaching me A-level history, endlessly insisted on a judicious, nuanced, on-the-one-hand-on-other approach to essay-writing saying: "There is no black-and-white, Jim-Jimmy, only shades of grey." I read out a kind of *belles lettres* effort written in this spirit, ending with a quotation from a Japanese researcher from my *Instinct* book which was roughly: "the cat has as much 'instinct' to love the mouse as to kill it." Much laughter from Nick and Keith, then Nick's comment that it was an "even handed" essay (more laughter), after which the two of them discussed the issue between themselves. The point is — one that took many years to sink in — that in the science of behaviour a theorist can be simply wrong. Yes the truth is complex in this science; but rarely a shade of *grey.*

It was not all as bad as this. This was my first exposure to the notion of "group selection," an idea that's treated as a relic these days, as modern biologists hold that it is the individual's genes that are selected for, not the group's (E. O. Wilson has recently revived group selection, to howls of scepticism). We — I really mean of course the other two — touched on V. C. Wynne-Edward's account of group selection (in a book Nick has been given by his landlady; "I know you work with animals") and on his idea of an "epideictic display." The latter referred to animals' tendency to congregate, as in the dawn chorus. Wynne-Edwards thought that they did so in order to estimate the size of the population, and that if it was too large they would refrain from breeding. I thought this was a wonderful idea. So there was an instinct for socialism! It was, I decided in my judicious and *belles lettres* way, "an interesting point of view" (we will return much later to the big issue of how one might explain the evolution of altruism given the "selfishness" of genes).

The Mind did not feature much in prelim philosophy either, with formal logic being a hard nut to crack. There was plenty of relevance to the mind, though, in the competence-capacity sense, in learning how to translate into the symbolism of the predicate calculus sentences, like: "candy is dandy but liquor is quicker," or "no man respects a man who does not respect himself" (Bede Rundle's examples in his excellent lectures to hundreds of prelim philosophy students). Perhaps the mind does this, or something like it, in understanding and producing sentences, something like a symbolism of *thought* underlying all languages. Or maybe these are just empty formalisms of no relevance to actual human thinking. There are big issues here to which we will return.

Rats and representation

Prelims over, I got down to the nitty gritty — experimental psychology. As Keith was at Trinity rather than Lincoln he left us for a Trinity-based supervisor and Nick Mackintosh supervised me solo on animal learning. This was the point at which I began to cease worrying about the distance of all this from The Mind and just enjoy what was on offer. I recall a conversation with Keith about the absence of "The Mind" in Oxford psychology. In Keith's view, psychologists like Nick thought they were moving towards an account of consciousness. I didn't believe that for a second, for there was no need to have such a terminus in the back of one's mind to ask questions about learning and conditioning in laboratory animals. These questions, while being *sui generis* to some degree and interesting in their own right, simply cannot fail to be relevant to human psychology. Humans have mammalian brains too.

Something else that could not fail to be relevant to human psychology, or to one's conception of it, was witnessing, in Nick Mackintosh's practical class in the summer term, his conditioning of a rat to press a lever for food. Put like that it sounds boring. However there is nothing boring about the almost casual process of transforming, by the selective delivery of food pellets, a directionless sniffer-about to a seemingly goal-directed creature. The "seemingly" is important, because there was at that time at least one perfectly satisfying account of how this is achieved that makes no reference to goals and to their representation (see below) by the rat. In years to come my eventual colleague, Tony Dickinson,[16] would demonstrate that there is indeed reason to believe that the rat can, in some circumstances, be said to be a goal-directed representer rather than a habit-driven automaton. What was important to me in 1967 was the questions it spurred about "what is going on inside the rat" to make this possible. This was emphatically not a king-of the ghosts-style curiosity. And it was a very un-behaviourist kind of curiosity too. The true behaviourist is concerned only with contingencies between stimuli and "colourless movements" (in J.B. Watson's phrase). There was not even much curiosity about what happened in the rat's brain from that kind of behaviourist. And this spurs two thoughts: one about what the term "behaviourist" actually means; and about the way in which the word "representation" came to feature in the vocabulary of animal learners — indeed in all of us — after the 1960s.

In the first place, some non-psychologist readers may have the idea that people like Nick Mackintosh who study learning in laboratory animals do it because they are "behaviourists" who think that all that needs saying about mammal mentality — the human variety too — can be said in terms of stimuli, responses, and reinforcement. Not so. There are many reasons

---

[16] See: A. Dickinson (1985) Actions and habits. *Philosophical Transactions of the Royal Society of London*, 308, 67-78.

for studying animal learning and none of them springs from a desire to reduce human behaviour to the above behavioural trio. How organisms learn is an autonomous question. Some animal learners may indeed have real behaviourist instincts. They may, for example, agree with B. F. Skinner that the human capacities, of which I spoke earlier, can be fully explained in terms of instrumental conditioning (the kind I witnessed in 1967). Of course, processes unearthed in animal laboratories are hardly going to be irrelevant to human learning. I repeat: how could they be when human and rat brains — let's not worry about octopi whose learning abilities Nick also studied — have a similar structure, though not power and complexity? We will see the evidence for this when we get to the mid '80s and to the rise of "connectionist" models of language and concept learning, associative models whose resources were not radically different from those used by Pavlov to explain a dog's salivation to a bell. In any event, during this time Nick was working on selective attention in rat discrimination learning and writing a major paper on this, which would later appear in *Psychological Bulletin.* Nothing could be less behaviouristic than an interest in attention.

As for the second spurred thought, it seems to me that once you use the term "representation" you are doing psychology in earnest. This is not to say that *all* behaviour, animal and human, must be explained by reference to how the past, future, and present are represented by the subject. For example, if, blindly following an habitual routine, somebody puts sugar in the washing machine's powder drawer, absently putting on a load of washing on while holding a bag of sugar bound for the cornflakes, this is due to a *failure* to represent the present goal. What's more, representation does not necessarily have to be thought of, or known about, in neural terms, because ideas about what goes on in the brain during the process of mentally operating on representations will come to us from behavioural theory and experiment. This latter must precede any digging about in the brain. Enough of this sermonising and back to 1967.

Each week I wrote an essay on some aspect of animal learning. In those days the student-friendly text books on (what was then called) learning theory did not exist[17] so one had to read about (say) Clark Hull's "fractional antedating goal response" (not goal *representation*, note) in Hull's own journal papers, gazing through the window of the Radcliffe Science Library onto the summer of love in a state of intense puzzlement. In fact, I found animal learning compelling, with the puzzlement continuing in a more comfortable way when I was just walking around, as out of this puzzlement arose what I liked to think of as my "own ideas."

What this amounted to in practice was my whisking up a hopeful coda at the end of each essay and stubbornly defending it in the tutorial. I rediscovered an argumentative streak dormant since the 6th Form common room. Two examples. I think I recall a receptive female rat in a goal box whose genitals had been sewn shut. The male rat worked hard to get there *nonetheless*. Under the (Hullian?) theory being discussed, the incitement of sexual desire was itself reinforcing.

---

[17] Donald Broadbent's fine book, *Behaviour,* is a possible exception.

I wasn't having any of this, for there were only a handful a
female undergraduettes in Oxford in those days many of whom
wore mini-skirts and some of whom wore purple and yellow
hooped tights as well and none of whom had ever been out with
me. Surely, I insisted, this was aversive — in *some* way. "But
what about nude books!" said Nick. Although I "smiled and
said nothing," like Tom the Cabin Boy, I must have been
thinking of their role in inducing a fractional antedating goal
response, which subsequently would be brought to fruition by
the agent himself.

The second example is from our final tutorial. The topic was
the phenomenon of "partial reinforcement," which is when an
instrumentally[18] conditioned rat only receives a food pellet
after every few lever presses rather than after every press. In
this case it will take much longer to "extinguish" the response,
meaning for the rat to stop responding altogether when the food
ceases to be delivered. There are associative and drive-based
theories — whatever happened to "drives" in psychology by
the way? — that can explain this phenomenon, but I like to
think that mine was a cognitive one. Partial reinforcement
leads to slower extinction phase, I reasoned, because a rat that
has received partial reinforcement will find it harder to
perceive/appreciate when extinction has begun. Nick
presented me with all the reasons why this is not a good idea,
and I stuck to my guns — a.k.a. did not listen and kept
repeating my point. When the hour was up he said: "I will
leave it to your conscience to decide who won the argument."

---

[18]   The animal is given food after responding.

He then told me that this would be all from him as he had
accepted a research professorship in Dalhousie University in
Canada. Next year my college tutor would be Dr Alan Cowey
– a physiological psychologist. I could not suppress a grimace
(commented on) at the word "physiological" — my only
science qualification being General Science O Level — but all
turned out well.

Brains, Bowlby, Bryant, and Big Theories

Alan Cowey was a gentle, cooly kind, meticulous tutor. He had
moved to the Oxford department from Cambridge with the new
Professor and Head of Department Lawrence Weiskrantz,
together with a number of other people, including Nicolas
Humphrey. "Weiskrantz–Cowey-Humphrey" is a triumvirate to
conjure with when it comes to the phenomenon of (what might
be called) unconscious vision. To explain: Nick Humphrey had
originally discovered in Cambridge that when a monkey's
visual cortex is removed it remains able to find its way around
the laboratory, avoiding obstacles and getting about, as if there
was still some kind of vision remaining of a sub-cortical kind.
Later, with patients who had suffered strokes that destroyed at
least half of the visual cortex, Weiskrantz and Cowey showed
that much the same is true of humans, and more dramatically
so. That's to say, a patient will insist that he is blind and yet
when asked to take a guess about the location of a stimulus in a
grid he will be better than chance. While this result has had its

share of brickbats (mainly of a statistical kind), the phenomenon of what Weiskrantz came to call "blindsight" is now well established.

In 1967, however, all this was a long way off. Alan tutored me in vision and physiological psychology (this was the original term for what we now call "neuroscience") and also gave me a tutorial on maternal deprivation (meaning the short- and especially long-term consequences of a child's being deprived of maternal care). I have no idea why Alan had expertise in this. I have put it down to the fact that the Cambridge system of tutoring ("supervising" in Cambridgespeak), unlike the Oxford one, usually requires the tutor to be a generalist. In Oxford, psychology tutors tutor only in their own research subject; in Cambridge a supervisor (tutor), if a fellow of a college, is expected to cover the psychological waterfront in years one and two.

From his research on juvenile delinquents and from looking at the way in which young children in hospital protest when their parents leave, then withdraw into themselves on the parents' return, John Bowlby came to the view that care by the *biological* mother was at least as vital to personal development as is vitamins to physical development (his analogy). Bowlby's research logic — looking back on the early experiences of a population of so-called "affectionless characters" rather than sampling more widely — can be questioned and his conclusions were too extreme. That said, his influence was, on balance, for the good. Yes indeed, taking a Bowlby view of development will increase a mother's feelings of guilt as she puts her child up for adoption; but under his influence the care of children has improved. When I was 18 months old I went into hospital for a hernia operation, during which time my parents were allowed to watch me bawling the place down through a glass-topped door. Nowadays the mother stays — thanks to Bowlby.

Bowlby was broadly correct that if a child is deprived of adequate early care there will be bad consequences for the later personality. But, he insisted that this deprivation means the *breaking* of an already-established bond between mother and child rather than the child never having had the opportunity to establish a bond in the first place. It is this latter that tends to do the damage, as Michael Rutter was to argue some years later.[19] So why did Bowlby argue for the former? Because his primary theoretical influence, in addition to Lorenz's research on imprinting in precocial birds, was Freudian theory — by way of Anna Freud. On the Freudian view, the trauma caused by the breaking of the bond causes an aggressive reaction that goes underground as an unconscious determining force. The exact form the Freudian machinery takes is not important for now. What's interesting is how a charismatic theory came to determine the project, despite the fact that for every tonne of Freudian theory there was a gram of heavily interpreted evidence. I'm not saying that this is unique to psychology. It's surely rife within it though.

At which it is natural to wonder: why a digression to John Bowlby only to end with such a decaffeinated point? Because it leads to thoughts about whether a grand psychological theory

---

[19]   In his book *Maternal Deprivation Re-Assessed*

is needed here *at all*. Is it not sufficient to examine the long-term sequelae of the different kinds of deprivation ("loss" versus "lack") for different kinds of disorder (psychopathy or depression) without regard to *any* major psychological theory? The answer is surely yes, and this because we are not psychological blank slates. We carry around with us theories of how early events lead to states of mind. I am not arguing here for the cracker-barrel wisdom of common sense,[20] because it is not held in common. People differ in their intuitions; and that's enough to get the empirical ball rolling. For some reason, we seem to feel the need for an external, big-time, challenging (to common-sense beliefs) theory to prop us up. Why? Not, I think, because psychoanalytic theory is king-of-the-ghosts psychology, but because the same instinct that leads to king-of-the-ghosts psychology leads us to feel we must work within Big Theories of The Mind. We fail to trust ourselves to get along without them. And let's not forget the baleful (is that word ever used without the next one?) influence of the psychological theories that sprang from Bowby. An example of this is the "bonding doctrine," which is the idea that if a mother is unable to cuddle her baby straight after birth — for whatever practical reason — and establish a "bond," then her maternal feelings do not develop. I recall seeing in 1973 a *New Scientist* article called something like "Maternal deprivation at 10 minutes after birth?" Having a medical emergency postpartum is bad enough, and now this! Yes, so "the psychologists" tell us.

[20] For a defence of the view that much of psychology is indeed common sense see: R, R. B. Joynson's *Psychology and Common Sense* (London, Routledge, 1974).

In contrast to what happens in many other universities, including Cambridge, the lectures, courses and the tutorials followed independent courses, touching only by good chance. Given this, Alan organized tutorials for me on all kinds of things with the lectures being more a source of stimulation than of teaching. I went to the lectures I enjoyed, more than to those I needed; irrespective of whether I could actually follow them. By far the most stimulating and impressive were those by Jeffrey Gray. He was a phenomenon, a running fount of enthusiasm and brilliance. A lasting image of him is his stepping over a wall rather than enter through a gate. This was long before the sober-suited Gray, who inherited the Chair of Psychology at the Institute of Psychiatry from Hans Eysenck in later years. This was the Gray of the black jeans, side-burns, and a distressed sloppy-Joe pullover, building week-by-week a black-box model, in talk and chalk, of the orienting system in the rat brain (think hypothalamic theta, enthusiasts). By "black-box" I mean psychological theories in which boxes with words in them like "sensory store" and "comparator" are linked with arrows, not necessarily in the hope that the boxes' contents will someday come to refer to brain loci. Jeffrey Gray said at the outset that this would ambiguously be a lecture course on the CNS — not just central nervous system, but *conceptual* nervous system (the arrows and boxes).

He was both teaching and sharing, asking the audience to suggest acronyms for the black boxes — "L for long-term potentiation?"(a female student said)… "Why not L for love?" (Gray said). Evgeny Sokolov, whose work formed the foundation of Gray's research, once popped his head round the door when Alan was teaching me. Alan Cowey did not tell me to go to the Gray lectures; though he went himself.

Another notable figure was Patrick (Pat) Rabbitt, who had also moved across from Cambridge with Weiskrantz. In those days the field of human memory suffered from a dearth of interesting theories, and it would be years before ideas like episodic memory (Endel Tulving – more on which much later), and working memory (Alan Baddeley and Graham Hitch) were to add some three-dimensionality. We were then lumbered with the simple and essentially false idea that there is short and long-term memory and that items move from the former to the latter by rehearsal. There were though lots of experiments and quite a few well-attested phenomena (like the primacy and recency effects); and so one could tell interesting stories so long as one stayed close to the data and kept the relevant plates spinning. Pat Rabbitt did this well, and that is why his lectures too were popular. They were tightly logical in the way of animal learning and analytical philosophy, and always with some spin of wit. When discussing the idea that memory gets worse with age because of increasing noise in the nervous system he said, nodding to Yeats, that one becomes "old and grey and full of noise." Actually this wasn't really my cup of tea. Though it was a pure form of experimental psychology, a kind of psychology that had evolved continuously from Ebbinghaus and his "consonant, vowel, consonant trigrams."

Peter Bryant's lectures were different again. They would set the course of my life; though the beginning was a little inauspicious. This was, I believe, Peter's first ever university lecture, and it was about as slow as it was possible to be without lapsing into silence. I assume in retrospect that the lecture course was on cognitive development, because in it I heard the name "Jean Piaget" for the first time. Not only heard it, but I saw it chalked, painstakingly, in letters about two feet high. As far as I recall, the first lecture was devoted to telling us about Piaget's famous "conservation" task — the conservation of liquid in this case. If anything justifies Alison Gopnik's[21] jibe about developmentalists' "neurotic task fixation" it is this one; and yet despite the tens of thousands of published studies purporting to nail down why children below 7 or so fail it we are now hardly the wiser. Children between about 4 and 8 years are shown two identical glasses filled to the same level with orange juice. The contents of one of the glasses is then poured into a taller, thinner container, and the child is then asked whether there is the same amount to drink in the untouched one and the tall-and-thin one. "No," children below 7 or so say: there is now more to drink because it's taller. Is it *really and truly* more? "Yes." Will you have more in your tummy if you drank the tall one? "Yes." A little boy just before you said it's still the same amount to drink because the level's only higher up and the glass is thinner, so do you still think there's more to drink in that one? "Yes." Why do they do this? This was not the kind of question I thought psychology would address, and yet I found the whole idea of thinking about the thought of children attractive. For one thing, children were psychologically as far removed as it is possible to be from the ultra-knowing public-school hippies who surrounded me. As it

---

[21] A major developmental theorist on whom I will touch later.

happened though, I could not attend the subsequent lectures as they clashed with some by Peter Strawson in philosophy.

In the next term Alan Cowey advised me to go along to another series by Peter called "Learning and the transfer of learning." I went under a cloud of scepticism. Surely this would simply be a bunch of experiments about what happens when you give learning tasks designed for rats to children. I was captivated. In these lectures big theories crumbled before Peter's gentle probing. They were faster than the first series, but still slow enough to give you time to ponder in the interstices. There was a boyish, hesitant charisma. He said (roughly) at one point, "We really must get on...I asked a colleague about how much he gets through in his lectures [laughter from PEB and audience]...So, let's crack on. As I said when I first told you about transposition, and that seems a very long time ago now...In fact, it *was* a very long time ago."

So, transposition. When studied in rats and pigeons this is known as "peak shift," and it is the apparent demonstration that these animals transfer what they have learned on the basis of abstract relations like "bigger," "brighter," "longer," more tilted to the right," and so forth. Here is an example with size. Let's say a rat is trained to respond to a 6" square rather than a 4" one. It succeeds to a criterion. Is this because it has learned to pick the bigger one or is it simply that it has learned to respond to things that are 6" square? One way to test this is to present it next with an 8" square plus a 6" one. If it has learned the relation is will pick the 8" one and if it has learned to pick the thing that is 6" square it will pick that one. Well, it responds to the bigger one (8"). But *has* it learned the relation "bigger?"

No, because if you then present the animal with a 12" square versus a 9" one it will respond randomly. There are a number of ways of explaining why the rats do this, and they are couched entirely in terms of associative strength. Children behave in much the same way till they are around 6 years, after which time they do indeed respond in terms of relations. Why do children pass the first task (called in developmental psychology the "near" transposition test) and fail on the second one — the "far" transposition test? One influential theory still around at that time was one in terms of language development. Margaret Kuenne argued, in the behaviouristic spirit of the time (1948), that as children acquired the language of size or brightness, or whatever, these tokens functioned as internal stimuli and responses — response "chains" – that enabled the older children to generalise in terms of relations rather than absolute amounts. It was the brute amount of linguistic experience that Kuenne had in mind, not any kind of endogenous improvement in linguistic skill. "Well," said Peter in his lectures, "of course 6 year olds have had more linguistic experience than 4 year olds, *but they have also had more food.*" More seriously, a theory like this "leaves unanswered" — as he put in his first book that would appear in 1971 — "the awkward question of how they learned the word in the first place." I have to admit that the bit about having more food reverberated in my memory, whereas the profound point about the "awkward question" passed me by at the time; because in those days I was terribly keen on the whole idea of development being driven by linguistic experience.

Why "profound"? As the philosopher Jerry Fodor was to argue a number of years later,[22] quoting with great approval Peter's point, if you want to argue that conceptual development depends upon learning the words for the concepts then you are going to have to accept that, in order to learn these words, the child will need the requisite representational format to understand their meaning — and this will be the concepts themselves. And this, for Fodor (and Plato), entails that "all concepts are innate."

So, I was keen on the very idea that Peter was arguing against, which is the idea that socio-linguistic experience is what makes cognitive development possible. In fact, I came across this idea from tutorials with Peter himself. It was Lev Vygotsky's central claim. I went along to St. John's once a week for five weeks, writing essays on "thinking" (this meant Vygotsky), Piaget, Freud, intelligence, and schizophrenia.

Now for two digressions: one about the teaching in those days; and one about why the grand theories of Vygotsky, Piaget, and Freud are *not* within the king-of-the ghosts domain (more precisely, the *authors* of these theories are not). First, back in the dark ages of the 1960s lectures were essentially talk and chalk, mimeographed handouts were a rarity, and the textbook industry had yet to begin production. In tutorials you were given a list of about four or five references, almost invariably to the original texts, and your struggles with these were, if not always rewarded, at least put to rest in the teaching hour. The result was that the essays produced were probably

---

[22] In his book *The Language of Thought*, more on which later.

less achieved and wide-ranging (and more confused) than those produced today. Yet the knowledge acquired through reading and discussion felt like — it almost was — one's own knowledge. I read Vygotsky's little book, *Thought and Language*, and it felt like a private discovery. Meanwhile in philosophy, I followed the journal debate between Russell and Strawson on the problem of linguistic reference, and it paralleled the difference between live theatre and a sitcom episode with canned laughter. One did not tap into resources; one almost constructed a perspective. At least this was the situation if you were lucky in your tutors, which I, with one hideous exception (see below), was.

Now to the Big Three: Vygotsky, Piaget, and Freud. It is pretty clear why the first two were not talking about the "essence" of the mind (king-of-the-ghosts style), but about the kind of process that makes cognition possible. Vygotsky and Piaget had in common the view that this was a process of *internalisation*: of social interaction becoming solo thought (which is dialogic) for Vygotsky; and of physical interaction with objects and with other children who view the world differently from oneself for Piaget. Surely though, Freud is a different kettle of fish. Was he not telling us that beneath the conscious mind there is an unconscious one like the conscious one except in its being unconscious, that we have poor access to our real motives, that we are the constant victims of a harsh mental censor on the one hand and brutish desire on the other? Is this not a psychology of "what we are like?" No. For my money at least, Freud was trying to explain how we "keep it together" in the teeth of biologically-grounded desires that would otherwise torture our everyday existence, destroy civilized society, and wake us from sleep. We do it, essentially, through defence mechanisms, dreams, and more generally by unconsciously driving beneath the conscious level.

One might also say that Freud stands apart from the other two because of his weak evidential base — already mentioned. He does. To put it mildly though, the evidential base for Vygotskyan theory is weak too, and Piagetians never really face up to a certain "awkward question" which is that the theory has to predict that motor impairment in early life should impede mental development;[23] and it does not.

I enjoyed Peter Bryant's tutorials immensely. I do, though, wonder if *he* enjoyed them. I would remove my sheepskin "flying" jacket, lay it on the floor, offer him a cigarette ("I don't thanks"), light one for myself, then read out an essay in which some opinionated coda received a whipping-up on nearly every page. Now these codas spread across the whole essay when intelligence and schizophrenia were covered; and this because of two authors Peter had suggested I read: Liam Hudson, for the first; and R. D. (Ronnie) Laing for the second. Hudson's second book, called *Frames of Mind,* had just been published. In this book and in his earlier *Contrary Imaginations* he more or less cheered on creativity against intelligence and, despite lip-service to scientific balance, also cheered on — these were his coinings, not as bad as "lateral thinking" but getting there — the "divergent" versus the

---

[23] This point is very well made by Margaret Boden in her little Fontana Modern Masters book on Piaget. It also cropped up the *Bois de Boulogne* debate between Piaget and Chomsky that I will discuss in due course.

"convergent" thinker. There was an undertow of Freud here, too. I recall Peter Bryant's slight smile when I recounted the view that, according to Hudson, the convergent scientific thinking is such because of repressed aggression. This was right up my street. And right up a lot of people's streets in those days was the work of Ronnie Laing.

Laing and Laing's lure

I decided not to research the autobiographical section of the book in order to keep my memory untainted by late-middle-age sensibleness. This helped my memory of Laing's *The Divided Self* to glow like a wonder. After all this experimental psychology, the phototaxis, the primacy effects, the juice-pouring-into-tall-glasses, here was a true psychology, a psychology about peoples' inner lives and how they can go wrong — so wrong that they might be diagnosed with schizophrenia. "False self system," "ontological insecurity" all stirred up with Dostoyevsky, Blake, and lashings of existentialism. What's not— as they say — to like. Yes, all kinds of people read Laing in those days. Indeed, a few months later I found myself discussing with my occasional philosophy tutor from Balliol, Nick Dent, Laing's newly minted book *The Politics of Experience and the Bird of Paradise*. I enthused, while Nick found what Laing described as a "psychedelic voyage of discovery in which the boundaries of perception were widened, and consciousness expanded," an embarrassment. Phrases like "self-glorifying garbage" spring to mind at this distance. How much of this is coloured by Laing's painful fall from grace? And how much of it is coloured by Laing's appearance in two *romans à clef*— Erik Jong's *Fear of Flying* and Clancy Segal's *Zone of the Interior*? And if these don't do the trick, how about his arrest for smashing an off-licence window, and his subsequent heart-breaking appearance with Anthony Clare on Radio 4's *In the Psychiatrist's Chair*? And perhaps the worst of all, his confession that while he denied drugs to his patients he himself was taking antidepressants. What point am I making here? Only that it is all too easy to despise Laing. For the purposes of this book he may indeed be a siren figure who lured this over-serious undergraduate onto the king-of-the-ghosts rocks, but he was a brave man. I think too he was entirely sincere. But more important, he did help some of his patients. Many conventional clinical psychologists respected him for that. It was an unconventional kind of help, and yet he put himself out. His life was not just a round of getting drunk with William Burroughs and being interviewed by the hippies from the *International Times*.

At home in the long vac I watched Laing being interviewed by the philosopher Brian McGee for a program called *Men* (this was 1968) *of Ideas*. "I thought he would look like an artist," said my mother. Dark-suited, he was low-key almost to the point of being withdrawn, saying a string of unexceptional things.

Peter was not a fan of Laing. He knew something of Laing's activities though, which involved a lot of (roughly in his words) "getting one group of patients to vote on whether they would meet another group." In any event, even I didn't entirely adopt the Laingian viewpoint. In the same essay-week Peter had me read about Peter Venables' experiment-grounded, cognitive work on schizophrenia. On this view, schizophrenia is a disorder of attention, an inability to filter out irrelevant stimuli. Actually, I was attracted to *both* kinds of approach.

Why lump Hudson and Laing together as king-of-the-ghosts psychology? It's not that they were "unscientific" in any simple sense. Hudson's work on IQ testing was perfectly scientific, and Laing's claims about the role of the family as a causative factor in schizophrenia were perfectly empirical and perfectly testable (and indeed they receive some empirical support).[24] It was that they were trying to tell us something about the essence of human nature: we have a neglected creativity; and we live under the threat of ontological insecurity. It is telling us about essence, while at the same time finding it impossible to do this without also telling us how to live our lives. For if you think you know about people's true nature and about how they can fail to realise it you will tend to tell them what *ought* to be the case psychologically. We all knew whose side Hudson was on when it comes to convergent-versus-divergent thinking; and Laing never tired of pontificating on good versus bad mentality. One extreme example of the latter is from an interview in the *International Times* in which said that if we fail to feel, at the point of

---

[24] Relapse rate is higher when patients are returned to families high on the E (for emotionality) scale, a scale that taps how critical the family is of the patient. See Marom. S. et al (2005) Expressed emotion relevance to rehospitalisation in schizophrenia over 7 years. *Schizophrenia Bulletin., 31,* 751-758.

orgasm, that one's self is flowing into the other then there must be some impairment in our mind-body relationship. And if — to zoom forward —you think that this is just late-'60s eccentricity then look at the present-day pontificating of those who work on the "psychology of happiness " — available from any Sunday newspaper, and dressed up with correlations. It is simply the rabbit who thinks he is King of the Ghosts. In my opinion, Laing had an excuse and the happiness researchers do not. After all, his views developed from trying to enter the world of the schizophrenic so as to render it meaningful, whereas the happiness researchers talk down to us from the rickety towers of pseudo-science.

Philosophy seeping in...and Chomsky

Returning to the late '60s I have had little to say about the philosophy side of things, and this because the kinds of questions asked in psychology and philosophy were usually orthogonal (no, the "psychological refractory period" — a tutorial from Pat Rabbitt — is not notably relevant to Hume on our knowledge of the external world). When, though, it came to Wittgenstein-and-Vygotsky, when it came to Piaget-and-Kant — each pair of them covered in one term, by sheer chance, it was like a light coming on. The Wittgenstein-Vygotsky axis was by way of the fact that they both grounded mentality in social practices. In his later work, one of Wittgenstein's targets was the idea that thought is a "private."

Of course it *is* private in the sense that thoughts are not broadcast, but it is not private insofar as the words in which we think do not gain meaning — do not have their reference secured —by private processes. That is to say, even for words that refer to sensory, emotional and mental states — words like "pain," "happy," and "think" — their reference is anchored not in a self-referential swivelling back of the inner eye to some raw experience. They are anchored in shared public practice. Meaning is secured by pain *behaviour* in one case, and by practical syllogisms, like: "It's in the cupboard, but if he *wants* it and *thinks* it's in the sink, he will look in the sink" in cognitive cases. As we have seen, Vygotsky too grounded mental "privacy" in public practice: in the early dialogues between children and others, as we have seen. This kind of view was my talisman from the late '60s for the next 25 or so years.

The Kant-Piaget axis is less obvious. Indeed, in his trilogy of books on infancy Piaget treats Kant as representative of one of the views he opposes — nativism (the view that the basis of human knowledge is innately represented). The parallel comes about via one of Kant's famous discussions of causality — in the Second Analogy section of *Critique of Pure Reason* — and from a single word that Stephan Körner used in his *Penguin* book on Kant to describe it. Kant wanted to oppose David Hume's view that all we know of causality is derived from the habit of mind involved in expecting physical effects to follow from physical causes (billiard balls colliding for instance). While Kant would certainly not put it this way, "beneath" this level, he argued that there is a more fundamental causal grasp which is the drawing of a distinction between sequences of perceptual experience that are under our control and those that are not. To take his own examples, in the first place (under our control), we may scan the front elevation of a house, and in so doing we are free to experience the elements in any order and to reverse the order — roof, front-door, second-floor window, and back again. In the second place (under the world's control) we watch a ship sailing upstream; in which case we see the ship on our left, then in front of us, then on our right. This order is not of our choosing and we cannot reverse it. In the book just mentioned Körner called the first kind of sequence "reversible" and the second kind "irreversible." Well, anybody with only a passing acquaintance with Piagetian theory knows that this distinction is its fuel and engine-house. Reversibility is the hallmark of thought and irreversibility is the hallmark of perception; and child-thought is inadequate insofar as it resembles perception.

I was, once more, lucky in having philosophy tutors who listened to my enthusiasms and, while not directly nurturing them, respected them: Harold Cox, the Philosophy Fellow at Lincoln; and James (Jim) Hopkins who had (I assume) a fixed-term college Lectureship. It's hard to imagine two more different personalities. And you could hardly imagine Harold anywhere other than Oxford. He was, though, a Francophile. In somewhere that was not Oxford (or, at a pinch, the Oxbridgey regions of London) or in France he would have seemed an exotic. Tall, bony, stooped, pipe-sucking, with something of Andre Gide about him, he carried an air of delicately insistent scepticism and total self-sufficiency. He had been a student of

J. L. Austin, the primary figure among the Oxford "linguistic" philosophers, who did philosophy by discussion, not by writing. This may be the reason why — in R. G. Collingwood's[25] phrase — he "refrained from publication." Though I like to think it was from an indifference to the whole process. He once said to me: "While I was shaving this morning I decided I was an emotivist about 'good' and a utilitarian about 'ought'." I was quite surprised and excited at one point when he recommended a book "by Don Lock, myself and others." I had misheard. Harold was not a co-author. The title of the book was *Myself and Others* — by Don Lock. Harold Cox taught me Kant, in addition to helping me to write English and to at least know what it means to think clearly.

Jim Hopkins was an American who had reached Oxford via Cambridge. He had — this the perfect phrase of my second wife Sally Barrett-Williams, who, before I met her, knew him when he was at King's London — "a double-jointed personality." I'll leave it at that. Charismatic and very likeable, he was a Wittgenstinian who gave the impression that getting clear about a philosophical problem was a matter of life or death. It was not unusual for him to bury his head in his hands as if confronting soul-busting grief, when in fact the issue might be as cool as our concept of "event." This was, though, absolutely not affectation; and at that time Jim was my ideal of an intellectual — D.H. Lawrence's selected poems on his desk and all. There was intensity. In discussing intention-in-speech he said at one point: "I may be arguing with my wife and say 'I

---

[25] His autobiography was called *An Autobiography*.

could kill you'." This was an example of how sentences need not be meant literally while still being meant. Intention in language use brings me round to Chomsky.

At that time Chomsky was delivering the John Locke lectures. I had gone along to them and reported back to Jim Chomsky's lampooning of the Wittgenstinian view of language in terms of social meaning. Chomsky told us that he had been giving a speech against the Vietnam war in front of a heavily-armed phalanx of the National Guard. He was not, he said, giving any thought to what the words meant: intended meaning was quite apart from inherent meaning; for *parole* was not *langue*.[26] His mind was elsewhere. Chomsky, Jim Hopkins said, was "philosophically naïve." Indeed this *was* almost a naïve observation on Chomsky's part because he and Wittgenstein were addressing completely different questions. Wittgenstein used the word "grammar" a lot, but this had almost nothing to do with Chomsky's interest in the machinery of syntax. It was all really a symptom of Chomsky's desire to take on all-comers. One that is still gloriously intact.

Before the first of his lectures there was a wave of people moving along the High Street towards the Examination Schools — the only building in Oxford big enough to accommodate Chomsky's audience — and I found myself walking behind a dapper business-man-like figure in a pin-stripe suit and carrying a document case (not to mention the short-back-and-sides). I recall thinking how frustrating it must be for him to be mixed up in this crowd. To my surprise the man turned smartly

---

[26] Saussure: the first is how we actually speak, and the second is our knowledge of language.

into the Schools to be greeted by Freddie Ayer... "Aaaah Professor Chomsky!"

I can't say I really saw the point of Chomsky in those days. For psycholinguistics tutorials (with the formidable Anne Treisman) I bought his *Syntactic Structures* – and gazed at it in puzzlement (my father, an upholsterer, joked on seeing its cover "I'm writing a book too — called *Tin-tack-tic Structures*"). The Chomskyan Revolution rumbled on without me.

I would bet good money that some future historian of psychology will try to show that really there was no such thing as the Chomskyan revolution. Well there *was*. You could tell it was a revolution, because so many people spent such a lot of time and energy combating his claims and failing miserably;[27] and these were big hitters like John Searle, not disgruntled no-hopers. Chomsky's central claim, which amounted almost to a philosophy of science, was that language, the core human faculty, is a form of tacit (= non-conscious) knowledge, whose nature experiments cannot unearth. However, linguists who employ the rationalistic strategy of arguing from the structure of what's to be learned (e.g., English) to what has to be present in the mind of the learner for this learning to be achieved (Universal Grammar), *can* unearth this basic structure — so he claimed. He was confident in his method, but not perhaps so confident in its ultimate success — as can be seen from the fact

---

[27] For example people who argued that we only "follow linguistic rules" when we speak in the sense that we follow the rules of mechanics when we ride a bike. We don't know the latter in the way that Chomsky said we know the former. The parallel between the cases is non-existent.

that he has been constantly and sometimes radically revising his theory till the present day.

I serve up the following anecdote in illustration of Chomsky's at-least-occasional lack of confidence in linguistics' ultimate success; and also of how he and the Wittgenstinians share a kind of mysticism about the mental, albeit a symmetrically opposing one. This is in 1971 when he was giving the Bertrand Russell Memorial Lectures in Cambridge; and it comes courtesy of John Eatwell,[28] one of his hosts. Chomsky was dining with Rab Butler, the Master of Trinity, on high table. Also present was the economist Piero Sraffa, who is credited by Wittgenstein in the preface to *Philosophical Investigations* as a strong influence: "…for many years increasingly practiced on my thoughts. I am indebted to *this* stimulus for the most consequential ideas in this book." Butler turned to Chomsky and asked: "So what is language Professor Chomsky?" — It is difficult not to be reminded here of the probably-apocryphal story about the taxi-driver who asked Bertrand Russell "So what's it all about then?" — To this Chomsky replied: "An unknowable property of the mind." Sraffa had been quiet up to this point. On hearing these words he put down his soup spoon and said firmly: "Then you should say nothing about it."

What's notable here is not merely the contrast with the synthetic confidence of the behaviourists who thought that "linguistic behaviour" is quite a simple matter really. It is that his faith in the notion of non-conscious "rules and

---

[28] Lord Eatwell is President of Queens' college, which I joined in 2006.

representations" was so profound that he thought it should be persevered with even if ultimate success was uncertain. It was, in the words of that most Chomskyan of philosophers Jerry Fodor "the only game in town." In any event, what Chomsky says about the language faculty seems to apply to the whole of psychology. We need to regard the mind as an interacting set of competences, or capacities as I have been calling them, with our goal being to explain the computations that underlie them, and to do this even if we have little confidence in our ultimate success. King-of the-ghosts-style, unreflective confidence is the enemy. And this brings me to my early experience of social psychology.

Social psychology — from Teddy boys and stand-up comics

I do not equate king-of-the-ghosts psychology with social psychology. Yes, while one is more likely to encounter king-of-the-ghosts psychology here than anywhere else a lot of social research is interesting; and if we can study social behaviour in animals then why not in humans? Social psychology is, though, and has always been, a kind of unanchored field, one propped up by a set of apparently compelling phenomena (cognitive dissonance, the Milgram experiment,[29] the Asch experiment, and so forth). This lack of confidence in the status of what one is doing day-to-day (not in ultimate success, *a la*

---

[29]   This will be discussed later.

Chomsky) can have bad effects. It can — as I discovered in one set of tutorials — breed a kind of aggressive-defensiveness, a nastiness rooted in lack of security. Or maybe Teddy Smaile,* as I shall call him, was just a nasty piece of work.

Let me, in passing, flag up the seeming contradiction between my accusing ghost psychologists of overconfidence on the previous page and now of lacking security in their views. This flip-flopping between extremes looks like a symptom of being un-anchored in reality.

This was the term in 1969 in which I had tutorials on social psychology. I was assigned to one of Michael Argyle's people. I say "people" in ignorance of whether he was a post-graduate student or a post-doctoral worker. In any event, he was a person difficult to admire. When I turned up with my first essay, ready to read it out, there seemed to be something in the air, as if I'd insulted him on a previous occasion. In appearance there was something of the Teddy Boy about him, not the full DA hair, drape and drainpipe, but certainly that aura. And he carried a verbal flick-knife. The first essay was on "the authoritarian personality," a concept owing to a member of the Frankfurt School of social theorists, Theodor Adorno. Adorno (a philosopher/sociologist) and his colleagues were trying to explain the psychological mechanisms underlying fascism, the psychology of those who did unspeakable things because orders had to be followed. The essential idea was that these were individuals who had suffered from harshly punitive parenting, causing them, in the Freudian style, to be be pumped up with unconscious aggression towards their parents. Their aggression could not be released by any normal route and so it was "safely" released, given the ideal circumstances, onto Jews, blacks, homosexuals, communists, and other out-groups. They obeyed orders because it was a way of letting off psychic steam. I read a descriptive essay on these ideas, ideas that, in some sense, were in good empirical shape. Individuals high on the F-(for Fascism) scale did indeed, for example, idealise their parents (the defence mechanism of splitting is at work here?). As I read, Teddy Smaile snorted or interjected with "Tuuhh!" and sneering laughter. Then after some surly, seemingly wounded questioning he treated me to his own take on it all. The whole idea of an authoritarian type was rubbish. It was simply a matter of low IQ. People with extreme political views (as if that was *all* there was to it!) were simply less intelligent. He may also have said that high performance on F-scale correlated with low IQ. I asked him what he then made of highly intelligent Oxford undergraduates reading Literae Humaniores who were Maoists. He laughed his laugh, and gave me the example of the *Daily Mirror* front pages: the readership (including me) of low IQ who had to be presented with simple and therefore extreme ideas like — these were his exact words — "Wilson's a cunt" — referring to Harold Wilson the Prime Minister.

This was shocking yes, but to my naïve mind *exciting* too. Here were real-world psychological issues confronted in a no-holds barred style. I was doing "real" psychology, which was… Well that thought didn't last to the end of South Parks Road. This was thuggish in style, and thuggish in content too. Things continued this way.

The next week I had to wait outside Teddy's room as another tutorial finished. On the hour, a young man — one of my fellow PPP students — emerged with tears streaming down his face. Teddy was shaken and pleadingly said to me more-or-less: "Well *you* can take it, can't you?" The following week and the week after he was up to his old tricks again. The topic was social skills, and social skills was, in those days, the central programme of the resident social psychologist, the pleasingly eccentric Michael Argyle — the man who was either Teddy's mentor or employer. Whereas nowadays we tend to think of interpersonal skills in terms of empathy and theory of mind, in the late '60s, perhaps from a behaviouristic hangover, it was regarded more in terms of overt skill — maintaining eye-contact, showing you are paying attention, responding appropriately. No doubt this was yet another something that would get Teddy's goat, so, as this was the final supervision with him, I thought I would go the whole interpersonal hog (to mix my animal metaphors) and lay some Laing on him. To this end, I borrowed from the Experimental Psychology library a book by Laing, Phillipson, and Lee called *Interpersonal Perception: A Theory and a Method of Research*. This was a recent book, only published a couple of years before. It was, in a sense, theory of mind[30] on turbo-drive and was to lead to Laing's book of sort-of poetry some years later called *Knots*. Laing et al was not so much a book of research as an illustration of how our beliefs about others beliefs (perhaps

[30] I will discuss theory of mind research later. One might say that Laing was ahead of his time in discussing the recursive embedding of "propositional attitudes" (e.g., think/hope/etc. that X) within one another.

about others' beliefs about our beliefs about them; with the same going for intention and desire) can tie us into interpersonal knots (of inauthenticity?). I ended my essay with a long quote from the book to illustrate my point that beneath the overt level of skill there lurks a mentalising tangle. When I had finished, Teddy fixed me with his you-poor-young-twerp smile and asked what I thought of it all, despite the fact I had just been telling him. He had nothing to say, because all he was interested in doing was demolishing before my very eyes the concept of social skill. "When we have a conversation," he said, " is it a matter of *skill* that we do it in the same room rather than from either side of a locked door?" — and so forth. His would-be Socratic questioning summed up to no more than: "Have-you-stopped-torturing-your-children?" bullying. By this time I had simply had enough of this creature and lapsed into silence.

Where is this located — you may well ask — in relation to the business of king-of-the-ghosts psychology? Well, the kind of psychology on offer here was certainly not the king-of-the-ghosts kind. For reasons given earlier, Freudian theory is not this because it tries to explain how we "keep it together," social skills research is, after all, about what we can do and how we do it, while cognitive dissonance research (another object of Teddy's blunderbuss contempt) is about self-deception, the thriving cognitive psychology of this has nothing ghostly about it.[31] What is of interest here is the phenomenon of Teddy

---

[31] Mijovic-Prelec, D. and Prelec, D. (2010) Self-deception as self-signalling: A model and experimental evidence. *Philosophical Transactions of the Royal Society B), 365,* 227-240.

Smaile himself — the very fact of his presence and character within one of the world's best psychology departments. Here was a prime example of the inflation of the rabbit mind into a King of the Ghosts. I wouldn't say that this inflation is *uniquely* afforded by psychology, as I said before; but it sure is afforded. My diagnosis is this: Psychology in general, and social psychology especially, leads its practitioners to believe that they have a special kind of insight into the human mind, rather as a plumber might have a special kind of insight into the water-management in your house. Given this, they "come to a view" — their precious perspective on what we are like; and coming to this view means dismissing, more or less *a priori*, other views from other rabbits. The less personally and intellectually secure the person the more chest-beating will go on. Rather than develop this point, which will receive a defence in the third part of the book, I will add a further something about Teddy to do some "developing" for me.

Some weeks later I met somebody, unrelated to psychology, who knew Teddy Smaile through a friend of hers. She excused his poor behaviour by the fact that he was going through a bad patch research-wise. He was collaborating on a project with somebody at Sussex University, a project on altruistic behaviour. They needed money to construct a piece of apparatus for a study that would pose the musical question: are people altruistic? *Are we altruistic?* If you want a king-of-the-ghosts question this certainly is it. I recall responding, in the (faux) hippy style that I thought impressed girls, "How could a *machine* answer that kind of question?" I may even have rounded off with "...*man*." My faux-hippy self was correct. Let us take a cool look at the question of altruism and how it sits in relation to ghost-psychology.

Altruism, on the appropriate (evolutionary biologist's) definition, is not just a matter of doing good to others, which is common and easy. It is doing good to others *at some cost to oneself,* even at the cost of one's life.[32] The obvious answer to the question of whether we are altruistic in this sense is "yes, people sometimes are." The answer that "no people ever are" would seem to be absurd — how could we possibly *know* this — and so the empirical question: "are people altruistic?" is itself absurd. At this point the ghost-psychologist sashays in with the thought that while people do indeed sometimes do good to others at a cost to themselves, there is in fact a benefit to them which is the self-satisfying glow of being a good person — of feeling good about yourself, and maybe actually boosting one's physical and mental health "according to recent studies." It's not just that this is cynical: it is scientifically useless, because irrefutable. It is not meaningless, and one would need to be a logical positivist to think it is; but it is empty of content. It means that any putative evidence for a genuinely altruistic act can be explained by the belief (it is no more) that the agent was self-serving. Even if the agent thought she was simply doing good the psychologist can say: "But my research/theory tells me that you have no first-person authority here. You are self-serving."

---

[32] Hamilton's Rule states that the probability of an animal sacrificing its life depends upon the genetic relatedness to the donor of the animals who will benefit and their number. Formally: rB>C where r means genetic relatedness, B is number who benefit, and C is cost to the donor. J.B.S. Haldane joked: "I would lay down my life for two brothers or eight cousins".

How do we get into such a twist? Because of the ego-inflation of psychology in which *The grass is full//And full of yourself. The trees around are for you,/ The whole of the wilderness of night is for you,/ A self that touches all edges.* It affords people like Teddy Smaile — and there are plenty more where he came from— the freedom to think they can tell us about ourselves, armed with statistics, a laboratory, and a middling intellect. While this may be going off the academic radar, sometimes the only response to stupidity is a visceral one.

Around the same time there was a series on lectures on offer called Theories of Personality, given by a visiting academic from North America called Fabian Klein.* In those days I saw "personality" as the kernel of psychology, and assumed that one had to crack the nut of the dry stuff to get to this, the meat of the matter. Here it was at last. I can't say I didn't enjoy these lectures: I enjoyed them as light entertainment. Klein was a good lecturer in that he held the audience and was fluent and sometimes funny; but it was entertainment only. It was Radio 2 psychology (or "Light Programme," as it was in those days). Here was the sex-crazed monkey in the cellar, the maiden aunt, and the rest of the Freudian cartoon show. Here was crass humour. Hysterical paralysis: an apocryphal spinster has her hand paralysed as if grasping a test-tube "as she has been engaged in mutual masturbation with the local vicar." Then after Freud and the post-Freudians came the American Pollyannas (Carl Rogers) and bores (Harry Stack Sullivan). As for the latter, there may be nothing inherently boring in "the significant other, " "the self system" and personality regarded in the context of "enmeshed" interpersonal relationships, but pour a little water on them and they blossom into first-rate bore-garden. It was when Klein started his reverential reference to HSS that I stopped going. We liked the "Stack" though; and I do recall one summer evening our trying it out with other names, aided by exotic cheroots: Mick Stack Jagger, Bob Stack Dylan ... Bob Danvers Stack Walker.

What was most irritating about Klein were his attempts to ingratiate himself with the audience by making digs at experimental psychology — methods and content (not to mention his occasional right-on references to being "stoned"). He assumed that we found, just as he pretended to find, the whole idea of a tachistoscope (a laboratory tool for flashing up words rapidly) inherently absurd and uncool. He introduced the work of one of the more lurid American bores by saying: "Now imagine you are lying beside the Cherwell reading a book on ... oh I don't know, *signal detection theory* (a mathematical algorithm for how subjects set the criterion for judging whether a stimulus is or is not present) and someone comes up to you and says: "why don't you try this instead." With this "this" being — I invent — Izaak Frankfurter's theory of self-hood as the psychic actualisation of the familial-erotic project. Well actually the audience probably *did* find signal detection theory more interesting that this puddingy guff; because intelligent people enjoy difficult things and ideas that have some empirical import. The only difficulty that Rogers, old Stack, and the Frankfurters present is that of staying awake to hear about them.

To give Klein his due, maybe he felt he had to be funny, because otherwise we would have died of boredom. You cannot sustain the attention of a bright audience for 50 minutes on a diet of intellectual pabulum, by which I mean theories undisturbed by evidence or conceptual analysis. At least the much maligned Eysenkian theory of personality,[33] which, if I recall correctly, Alan Cowey taught me —a theory as modern as classical conditioning and yet as old as Galen; indeed as old as astrology— was based on firm empirical grounds. By "firm," I don't mean true, I mean explicit and testable.

While personality is a straight-forward-enough concept, in studying it two faces are apparent: The Siren-face of ghost psychology, and the dull actuality. We can be drawn to personality because it seems to promise knowledge not only of what we are like in all our variety, but also the cognitive tools to assess people — for seeing through to what they are *really like* from this knowledge. The dull actuality is questionnaires and correlations, the apotheosis of which is market research (extroverts like this perfume so package it in red).

Disillusioned as I was becoming with social and personality psychology, I was still haunted. In short, buoyed up by my reading of Laing and Hudson, yet stiffened by my interest in Peter Venables' work on schizophrenia, I decided to do my final-year research project on the question of whether high-creatives (Hudson) find it more difficult to filter out irrelevant

---

[33] One of its central claims is that extroverts are less easy to condition (classically) than introverts, because the latter have a higher level of cortical arousal. His two-dimensional (introvert-extravert/stable-neurotic) theory of personality goes back to Galen (phlegmatic, choleric, sanguine and melancholic), indeed to astrology (Earth, Fire, Air, Water signs).

stimuli (a strange associative train here: from Venables to schizophrenia to Laing). What more could you want — creativity *and* schizophrenia. It was encouraging by the fact that Pat Rabbitt, who had kindly agreed to shepherd me through this, had a couple of William Blake prints taped to a filing cabinet. After all wasn't Blake both creative and — hey let's face it — a bit schizophrenic? In practice, I hunted around for volunteers who would take both Mednick's Remote Associates Test (a test of finding the common link between three words) and a timed test of counting stimuli on cards and sorting them into piles. Sometimes the stimuli were words, and people who were good at the RAT task were slowed up when it was words that had to be counted. All this meant was that wordy people can't help but read words (the consensus now is that RAT is simply a verbal test). I replicated the result some years later and published the study as a short report.

At this point (the summer of 1969 with Finals looming) many of my ghost-instincts were still intact, in the sense that my interest in psychology was framed within a vision of what humans are essentially like: creative, imaginative, socially-determined, thinking in natural language, and with ineffective linguistic thought lying at the heart of inadequate development and inadequate living. I had however managed some kind of divorce between psychology and literature, writing Kafka-lite stories and terrible poems parallel to my two essays a week. I did in fact submit one of these terribles — called "Thoughts on the Death of John Coltrane" and with Jabberwocky prosody — to a poetry magazine, published in my college, called *I Like You.* The editor was saved the job of rejecting it, because the magazine didn't run to a second issue. It would be 30 years before I published a poem in a magazine.

Critique of Pure Reason — the movie!

Scribbling aside, what was I to do after graduation? Two courses suggested themselves: pursuing the Hudsonian-Laingian line in some kind of research, or digging deeper into what I saw as the commonality between what Kant argued in the Second Analogy (p. 59 above) and what Piaget thought was a necessary condition for mental development. I applied then, on the first prong, to do an M.Ed. in educational psychology in Liam Hudson's unit at Edinburgh and to UCL and Birkbeck London to do a Ph.D. on the parallels between schizophrenic and child thought[34] (thoroughly steeped in Vygotsky, this). I had chosen UCL because of the presence of the psycholinguist Philip Johnson-Laird and Birkbeck because of the presence of Peter Venables. On the second prong I applied to the Oxford Philosophy Faculty to do a B.Litt. on Kant's arguments in the Second Analogy.

The trip to Edinburgh for the interview was enjoyable, despite my finding little tolerance for long hair north of the border (on stepping down from the train a porter cried out "Now look at *An*gela!"). I could not, though, see myself in Hudson's unit, nice as the people were who interviewed me.

---

[34] The idea was to start with the Hanfmann-Kasanin's Concept Formation Task, a highly elaborated version of a test developed originally by Vygotsky.

The place exuded naïveté; though maybe if I had met the boss I would have thought otherwise. UCL rejected me, with my receiving the rejection on the morning of my first finals exam; though Birkbeck accepted me, as did, once the Finals results were out, the Oxford Philosophy Faculty. I decided on Birkbeck for a number of reasons, not least of which was the prospect of being supervised by the psycholinguist Judy Greene, to whom I had taken a liking at the interview. It also meant living in *London*. With regard to philosophy, I thought: (a) I was far too impulsive and impressionistic a thinker to make a good philosopher; and (b) I could pursue that line within psychology.

Testimony to just how "impressionistic" I could be in relation to philosophy is given by the fact that soon after Finals I went off to mid-Wales to make a 16mm film of the *Critique of Pure Reason*. No, this is not a surrealistic add-on. Hard fact.

My parents had given me £50 for my 21st birthday present, and I thought this would be a good way to use the money — a lot of money in those days. My aim was something between German Expressionism (luckily the person playing Man could make-up and gesture like the lead in *The Cabinet of Doctor Caligari*) and Warhol (I would film whatever happened and nothing would be thrown away). Through a friend of a friend I met up with a guy from Brasenose called — check this out psychologists![35] — Conway Lloyd Morgan who helped to arrange casting and took us off to his parents' cottage in mid-

---

[35] This is Conwy Lloyd Morgan's (1852-1936) famous "canon": "In no case is an animal activity to be interpreted in terms of higher psychological processes if it can be fairly interpreted in terms of processes which stand lower in the scale of psychological evolution and development."

Wales (Builth Wells) to film it. I was Understanding (in subfusc) while other cast included, in addition to Stephen Zundell's Man, Receptivity, Lena the Goddess of Pure Reason, Imagination, Time, and of course Space, played by Howard Rogers, who would go on to produce the Radio 4's *The World at One*. Experiencing the world at sixes and sevens in mid-Wales may have helped prepare him for this.

I wrote some songs for the soundtrack, one of which posed the musical question of whether, in coming to apply the Kantian Categories in our thought, we had "lost the bright Bird of Paradise." Yes, it is possible to be a Laingian *and* a Kantian if you are sufficiently young-and-foolish.

London: Syd Barrett, the Birkbeck Timer, and marriage (three remote associates)

No I did not meet Syd Barrett in London, despite my haunting the Portobello Road in an overcoat made of muskrat fur. I did however spend a lot of time in my hall-of-residence room twelve stories above the Euston Road playing *The Madcap Laughs* and drawing up plans on a foolscap pad for my earth-rattling project of research. It would be at once clinical and developmental, Laingian and Vygotskyan, scientifically watertight — yet, you know… far out. Judy Greene would listen with a warm smile, knowing I would calm down eventually (I was, I have to admit, much enamoured of Judy. A big fan of the Warhol movies of the time, I saw her as a vivacious version of his superstar Viva…which feels like dangling a modifier). She wrote a letter to the British Museum supporting my application for a reader's ticket. The official story was that I wanted to become better acquainted with some of the more obscure phenomenological philosophers; though she knew the unofficial story, which was that I wanted to become better acquainted with an American girl called Jan

Lowen, who was doing research on Wyndham Lewis in the BM.

In any event, the stimulus to calming down came sooner than either of us expected. I visited a mental hospital in Tooting Beck along with one of Peter Venables' post-grads (John Gruzelier) and another first-year and female, post-grad. As it turned out, I was playing the gooseberry on that outing. This was not what disoriented me however. My romantic vision of the schizophrenic as someone between a psychic brigand and a guru of the inner world melted in those few hours. I met some of the inmates. I sat in the testing lab, in the EEG chair at one point, among the encrusted coffee cups left there by another Venables postgrad (Lawrence Warwick-Evans; called by Jan "Lawrence Warence") and decided I would never enter a mental hospital again, as a psychologist at least. I both lacked the mental toughness to take an objective view of mental illness and I did not wish to become hardened to it. The patients were overwhelming individually, and the whole was impossible. There was the plumy-voiced ex-headmaster who seemed perfectly sane if over-emphatic and eager to please sitting in pyjamas and dressing gown by the French windows; the emaciated man standing in a doorway who after a long contorted struggle would say a single word; the beautiful and tiny Indian lady who greeted us shyly in her padded cell as if we had come to tea, whose direct gaze was unbearable.

Anyway, there was little point in what I wanted to do with the patients, which was a concept-learning task done by block sorting based on one described by Vygotsky and one more rigorously developed by Hanfman and Kasanin (see footnote

34, page 76). My planned work was basically old fashioned, the drugs the patients were taking would grossly affect performance — I did wonder aloud if perhaps they might *please* be taken off the drugs so I could do my important work — and I was asking a naive question (about whether schizophrenic thought parallels child thought in being concrete and thematic[36] rather than abstract and taxonomic). As we now know, young children's concepts are perfectly taxonomic, especially if the tasks are presented in the context of novel language learning.[37] So the "optimum strategy" (a phrase often in use by Birkbeck's memory people) was to focus on developmental work only.

To nursery schools in Cecil Gee

It was good that Judy was not a developmentalist, as this meant I could go my own way. It was good; and it could have been bad. Her own research was on negation, and she was in the process of writing her excellent introduction to Chomsky and psycholinguistics for Penguin. I was still very far from being a Chomsky fan at that point and carried around with me a number of what I thought were industrial-strength arguments

---

[36] A thematic link is "ring-finger," a taxonomic link is "ring-necklace."

[37] Ellen Markman has shown that even 3-year olds can interpret words taxonomically – see previous note. See Markman, E. M., & Hutchinson, J. E. (1984) Children's sensitivity to constraints on word meaning: taxonomic versus thematic relations. *Cognitive Psychology,* **16**, 1-27.

against his ideas — against the very idea of his ideas. The only time our relationship came under strain was when it was Judy's turn to tell the new graduate students about her research. This was not the time to field these arguments, yet I did; and loutishly. When she showed us an article she had written for an architectural magazine exploring the parallel between Chomsky's ideas about the deep and surface structure of a sentence and that of a building (the basement and above-ground structures) the casual observer could have mistaken my face for that of Teddy Smaile.

So my thesis was to be on concept development in children. I had no overall plan, and would begin with the transposition experiment (see page 50) by shamelessly stealing an idea Peter Bryant had voiced in one of his lectures. According to Peter, young children are essentially relational learners, and that is why they pass the near transposition task. According to me, in my great wisdom, they are essentially absolute learners, which is why they fail the far test; which is to bracket the "awkward question" of why they pass the near test.

Peter did make the point in his lectures that the transposition design confounds the way in which children code stimuli with the way in which they transfer information to a novel pair. In illustration of this he showed how it was possible, using a design based on speed of learning, to compare the ease of doing an absolute task (target cards the same size) with the ease of doing a relational task (target cards bigger or smaller). I really don't want, as they say, to get into all this, because it's not particularly germane. I was though asking a question to which

Nature could say: "No, wrong." Nature did: the absolute task was no easier; and Peter was correct.

I had never tested children before; and these were, if not terrible, then certainly typical 2 year olds. It struck me then, and has thoroughly seeped into my views on child testing over the years, that it's naïve to think that when you ask young children a question they are doing *anything like* the equivalent of what happens when you question adults (zero originality must be claimed for this thought; though that doesn't prevent it from being ignored). It is not that children are simply inattentive: it is that Piaget was correct, broadly speaking, in describing younger children as "egocentric." I saw this in my grandchildren when they were under 5 (or so) and I certain suffered from it through all those nursery mornings in Clapton, Finchley, Camden … A child of (say) three only engages with you on her own terms. Of course, there can be questioning to and fro in the free flow of behaviour, but it is nigh-impossible to break into the child's cognitive agenda with a question that happens to interest you. What determines the child's response, in the words of John Flavell (the author of what is still the best book on Piaget's theory), is whatever is currently "up-front in consciousness." I presented the 2 year olds with pairs of cards of different sizes, and they had to work out which one they had to point to with their sticky little fingers to find the picture on the back every time (same size one or bigger one). Of all the many things that interest 2-year olds at any one time, the size of squares takes a back seat, well behind the questions of whether they will see a picture of a "jumbo" this time, whether the bigger cards are good for skimming across the room, and what is in the top pocket of the tester's herringbone Cecil Gee jacket.

I had been worried the children would find me a bit scary; and some did indeed take one look and run away. In any event, my natural diffidence and a kind of hangover from hippiedom ensured that (in the words of one nursery worker to another in my hearing): "The children are more frightening than Mr Russell."

What amazes me in retrospect is my confidence that all this would eventually lead to something. Before I escaped from the hall of residence to a shared house in Islington I told one or two of my fellow inmates what I was up to. They thought it was hilariously beside any possible point: "Is that *it*!" I knew my next move was to compare verbal and nonverbal performance on these tasks and also to do something similar with the conservation experiment; and it seems nothing short of a miracle now that I ended up with a few decent experiments and with something approaching a theory or the framework of one. The support I received at Birkbeck, and from Judy in particular, was to thank for this.

Birkbeck — not a ghost house

A word then about Birkbeck and about how it was in no way shape or form a host to the ghost. This was a place of experimental psychology more or less in the Oxford mould. There was animal learning, visual perception, and physiological psychology. Mainly, though, there was memory, or more accurately "verbal learning," or more concretely "learning lists of words or meaningless trigrams." Perhaps the star (though absent in Toronto for most of my time there) was Fergus (Gus) Craik. Many times I sat in the refectory at lunchtime as Craikians with or without Gus scribbled graphs and discussed the significance of the Peterson and Peterson study (preventing rehearsal by counting backwards in threes) and others like it.

For me, the essence of Birkbeck in those days could be summed in by The Birkbeck Timer. This was a piece of laboratory equipment for presenting stimuli to subjects and timing their response to them. My BPS (British Psychological Society) diary — this accompanied my everywhere, even when watching, in my fur coat, Rory Gallagher blow the roof off at a UCL gig — contained a diagram of it. I have, though, to own up that I thought this was just the kind of thing it was my business to transcend, as I delved into Stephen Toulmin's wonderful two-volume *Human Understanding*, read some rather less wonderful books of essays on phenomenology, and pondered exactly what Jerome Bruner meant by saying the conception of conserved amount in the Piaget experiment was analogous to Chomskyan deep structure.

Here is a shaming example of this kind of arrogance. A much-loved lab technician was retiring and there was a drinks-plus-presentation party for him one afternoon. His leaving present came in a large box, and I — wine having been taken — said too loudly to the person next to me "It's a Birkbeck Timer" — a comment that was pure Fabian-Klein-smart-Alec and one that embarrassed Judy nearly as much as it embarrassed me. If it had been within earshot of the head of department Professor Arthur Summerfield I would have been in real trouble.

Arthur Summerfield was a warm and dominating presence. His pugnacious side could serve the department well in university meetings when, whether on purpose or not, he would lose his temper. He once lost it with the graduate students when we (rather "they") presented him with some demands and whinges about the lack of graduate accommodation. We were arraigned before him for a most satisfactory and well-deserved bollocking: "You are *psychologists* after all!"

I suspect that it was Summerfield's drive and clear vision of Birkbeck as a bastion of experimental psychology that laid the foundations for its being the excellent department it is today. For me, in fact, Birkbeck was nothing more that a place I checked into from time to time to present Judy with my latest failed prediction and to act — this was expected of us — as a "demonstrator" in the practical classes. I lived in a bubble, with proof of this being that it took me about a couple of months to discover that Birkbeck's undergraduates were all *part-time* and mostly mature students (why did all the teaching take place in the evenings and why were most of the undergraduates older than you? Search me). You would have thought that even my Latin could have risen to the challenge of *In Nocte Consilium* chiselled on the front of the building.

I cannot claim to have been a roaring success as a demonstrator, and hated it when we had to design an experiment with a group of undergraduates. This dislike was partly fuelled by practical classes clashing with modern jazz night at my local pub. In any event, Birkbeck students were (or are) not noticeably deferential. Once when I tried to wind things up early a blonde, lanky know-all of a man I had seen around Islington said to the group: "He's got to get to the jazz at the *Rising Sun* you see" (I did. It was baritone sax player Ronnie Ross). The same guy simply walked out one week saying that he'd had enough. Neither was I roaringly successful as a marker of the project write-ups. Part of the problem was that they were better at statistics than I was, with the other part being that I simply could not be bothered. What's more, I would sometimes forget to turn up. On one occasion Vernon Greg, who ran the practicals, contacted me at home. When I had been fetched up from the basement I came to the phone and said — the phrase is memorable to me — that I would "undertake to promise" to turn up next week. I can't blame Vernon for refusing to write me a reference when it was time to apply for jobs: "I've never come across an attitude like yours before," he said. If Vernon Greg had been of a much older generation he might have said something like: "The time which Mr Russell can spare from the adornment of his person, he devotes to the neglect of his duties."[38]

There is no particular point to this spasm of self-flagellation. I can't even blame dope-smoking, which I abandoned in 1971 on taking up transcendental meditation — a sentence that has "early '70s" written all over it.

---

[38] The Master of Trinity, Cambridge, W.H. Thompson, in the late 19th century. He was referring to the classicist Richard Jebb.

Philosophers and five-year-olds

I mentioned my "bubble" just now, and this must account for why I never went along to see David Hamlyn in the philosophy department at Birkbeck. David was a philosopher who had written, and would continue to write, about Piagetian theory with great insight and clarity, from a broadly Wittgenstinian perspective. In parallel with my child testing I was reading up on what philosophers and psychologists who studied the theoretical foundations of developmental psychology — Stephen Toulmin (already mentioned), Bernard Kaplan, Harry Beilin, David, and some others — had to say about mental development. The general issue they addressed was that of conceptual change, an issue as old as Aristotle, as Hamlyn often pointed out. How is it possible to go from a state of little knowledge to a state of richer knowledge? Is innate structure necessary, and if so what kind, and how? More specifically, though, they were concerned with the status of Piaget's so-called "genetic epistemology." Never not ambitious, Piaget thought that the study of mental development would shed light on traditional questions about human knowledge. For instance, if Piaget is correct that infants "construct" their understanding of the physical world through action (see reference to Kant's Second Analogy – p.59 above) then will this not have implications for what it means for us to have knowledge of an external world? To the purist, Piaget was simply confusing empirical issues with conceptual ones. Yet Kant too deliberately blended the "synthetic" (true by experience) with the "analytic" (true by the nature of the concepts involved); and many philosophers, most notably W.V.O. Quine, would dispute the very distinction. So there was a lot to think about. I did eventually meet David some years later, though not in a very satisfactory context (a one-day conference on genetic epistemology in Manchester at which he was speaking and I was trying to). Life would have been easier if it had occurred to me to get out of the lift on a lower floor and go along to see him.

Quite apart from such highfalutin' stuff, I was working on what I saw as the centrepiece of my thesis, which was the demonstration — yes the demonstration, not the testing of the hypothesis — that the difficulties children have with tasks like conservation (p.49 above) were linguistic in nature. Here I saw myself as attacking Piaget with Vygotskyan battalions. Rather than devise a non-verbal test of conservation, which could in some way settle issue — this was to follow some years later — I waded into the crowded waters of the training study. Researchers, as Harry Beilin often pointed out, had indeed shown that while simply telling children what you mean by the question in childlike language may work for a few days, the children usually regress to being non-conservers and the training does not generalise to other kinds of conservation (e.g., from liquid to number). Verbal training seemed to have lead to mere parroting. As Peter Bryant was to say some years later, if cognitive development was that easy, why not just give them a couple of tutorials and get it over with. What I decided to do though was to investigate 5-year-olds' interpretation of conservation language ("same amount of room for X") independently of their conservation performance. They interpreted the phrase as meaning "same shape" when selecting a comparison object among others and as "same height" when producing a comparison object, *and they could not be linguistically "educated" out of these interpretations.*

I regarded this as the routing of my Vygotskyan forces, and recall sitting in a pub in Belsize Park one lunchtime over beer and sandwiches confronting a failure that some would describe as "existential." In fact, I had never bothered to think through Piaget's answer, which was also Jerry Fodor's and Peter Bryant's answer, to those who say that children's failure on tasks like conservation is "verbal." Of course it is verbal, Piaget would say: "They cannot understand the language because they cannot think the thoughts!" A Piagetian might go on: "Do you think you can bring about conceptual change by just *talking* to children? Ever tried doing this with adults?"

I certainly worked hard on my "verbal training" with these poor benighted 5 year olds. I don't believe I ever used the expression "If I've told you once I've told you a thousand times" when explaining to them that whether another "zoo" had "the same amount of room for the animals" as the initial zoo was not, I repeat *not,* just a matter of whether it was the same height or also square or also cuboid ... but I certainly thought it. So what *was* amount? This is the conceptual, never mind empirical, weakness of verbal training: it is no easy matter to explain exactly what words like "amount" mean. In my thesis I would go on to call concepts of the conservation type "rule-bound." That apart, my "working hard" was picked up by one of the teachers. "One hears that you can be a bit heavy-handed with the children Mr Russell" said the headmistress, having

called me to her study. I had not been trying to prove that I
could be at least as frightening as the children.

From the Rising Sun to Golders Green to Glasgow

Around the time of running my training study the research
became somewhat overshadowed by my personal life. One
evening I returned to the Islington house to find visitors. These
were people from another shared house that my housemates
had met that evening in *The Rising Sun.* There was a
discussion under way about why we had a plaque on the front
door saying: "The Islington Mime Troupe" (a would-be-droll
reference to what one of the American constituents, Clint,
thought of as our lack of real, or American-style, "verbal
communication"). The only spare seat was next to a petite,
big-eyed, bored-looking girl in a white PVC mac. I felt an
inevitability (even if Christine Carr did not) and we were
married within a year.

The upshot was that my thesis writing-up would be done in
our flat in Golders Green. Marriage does implant a seriousness
of purpose. We wanted a family and I would need a job ... so,
let's crack on. While Chris was at work in Holborn Public
Library I struggled to place my experiments within some kind
of theoretical structure, or at least a taxonomy. What I did was
distinguish between two kinds of concept, each of which could
be non-verbal or verbal: "rule-bound" concepts like those
tapped by conservation tasks in which at least two dimensions

are involved and non-rule-bound ones like those referring to absolute amounts and uni-dimensional relations. I persuaded myself I had shown that language is more intimately involved with the relative than the absolute ones of the latter kind, and held out the hope of demonstrating non-verbal competence in the rule-bound variety — nonverbal conservation in other words. It sort of worked, Judy was happy with it, and I felt I was good at this kind of thing as well as finding it satisfying. In fact, more creatively satisfying than the pastichey poems I would scribble off and on.

After a disastrous interview at Manchester Poly, at which I came to the view, and rapidly forgot, that drinking a lot of beer and whisky with friends in North Wales the night before an interview is not a good move for applicants of a nervous disposition, I was short-listed for a lectureship at Glasgow. Yes, and this with an incomplete Ph.D. and no publications — completely unheard-of now. I was delighted, and had very fond memories of Glasgow, which I had visited with my mother as a 4-year-old to holiday with her parents. Chris was less than sure she wanted to abandon London and a job she liked, but would be agreeable to it — almost "unheard-of-now."

I had already been sacked from two jobs (one as a schoolboy and one in the Oxford vac) and I had been a slacker-teacher at Birkbeck, so it felt like a minor miracle when I was offered the lectureship at a fine university (thank goodness my Auntie Katie had only doled out a single glass of *White Horse* the night before the interview). Immediately after the interview we drove up to Perthshire where my parents had rented a holiday cottage.

The central feeling about all this was that now I was free do get down to some real psychology. University lecturers were almost unsackable weren't they? Now I could study psychology as I wished, plumbing human nature rather than running dutiful experiments with sticky-fingered children.

I didn't belong to Glasgow— for long

"Any complaints?"

Immediately after the interview I'd been told to go over to the Psychology Department to wait for the Head of Department, Ralph Pickford, as they were planning to offer me the job before I left town. During my wait one of the lecturers asked if I would like something to read, offering me a book from his shelves. I was delighted to see they were all on personality. Yes, if I had to choose between Fabian Klein and the Birkbeck Timer it would, in those days, have been the former every time.

I might as well have had a predilection for Rosicrucianism, for all it mattered in the day-to-day. My lectures were only once a week (Tuesdays at 4.30) not day-to-day, and yet the very fact of having to lecture *at all* to 250 or so Diploma of Education students on developmental psychology was a fact that framed my waking hours, in and out of term, on Christmas afternoon, when sitting by Loch Lomond. The problem was simple: not only did I know almost nothing about the developmental psychology of the kind found in textbooks, but I just did not want to expose myself to people *who may not be interested.* My idea of university teaching was giving the benefit of my wisdom to people who were already two-thirds of the way there.

There are a number of ways of dealing with lecture-terror. One is to be immaculately prepared. The other — I did it *My Way* — is to fain indifference, adopt a devil-may-care, endearing, lackadaisical pose and William Brown-like insouciance, whilst all the time being scared witless. It's rather like — I self-deluded — the Olivier technique of getting into a role from the outside. And it's also rather like stupidity; because lecturing is not acting. The irrational rationale behind my technique was that if something went wrong it would not really matter; whereas if I were crisp and authoritative it would matter.

In fact, I did prepare the lectures quite thoroughly — though in a sort of open-ended or starfish manner with my notes scribbled on different sets of paper with instructions at the top like "go to p. 2A now!" I was like the man in the Roger McGough wise-crack who "aimed low and missed." How did I know I'd missed? because Glaswegians speak up — loudly, from the audience.

An extra-psychological instance of this speaking-up tendency arose when Chris and I went along one evening to the students' union (the *male* students' union in those days) during my first term. We'd gone to see Lou Reed. After the stunning first number (*White Light/White Heat*) there was a lull following the applause as Reed fumbled at his guitar with red-varnished nails: "Yurr a fuckin' idiot!" — from the audience.

Many of them may have thought I was exactly this during my early lectures; though nobody said it. When I mumbled at one point: "My notes are a bit disorganised I think," there was thumping of desks and cries of Yes! "Any complaints?" I said with a show of defiance. "Mr Russell, you seem to assume we know this already!" Thereafter it felt like me against them, and my stutter returned with a vengeance. While there were goodish days; in the bad days sweat seemed to be running down the walls. You can take it from me that when you are lecturing on Freud as a developmental theorist it is more than a little impeding if it takes you seconds to squeeze out the word "mother." I even had time to ponder both my career and my more immediate options during some attempts. Should I give this all up as a bad job? Should I try to make a joke of it and say, "father's wife?" Thank God I never did the latter (stutterers should never acquiesce as butts). The giving-up option was pondered intensively "off line," while keeping this crisis from Christine.

It was not all bad. I tried to present Freudian theory in a sympathetic way and more or less pulled it off. My idea was to give them what I called a "humanistic re-statement" of the theory; though really it was a metaphorical one. Accordingly, the father was the child's representation of authority and the socially refractory world rather than the literal dad; the mother was the child's representation of unconditional forgivingness and nurturance (something like the Virgin Mary, and certainly not the flesh-and-blood mum); the Oedipal stage was confronting the threat from the former that the latter could be lost if you languished in it; the spending of libido at the oral and anal periods was ...oh I forget now, something like overinvesting in the passive pleasures or the joys of wilfulness.

Adam Phillips may have seen some point in this, while Freud certainly would not. The audience seemed interested. In fact, the guy who had shouted the "know-it-already" comment gave me some drawings his child had done, which certainly had a rather Oedipal tone. I found the audience feisty, but magnanimous. Indeed, I don't think I remember anybody walking out from any of the 24 lectures: a far cry from Birkbeck's lanky know-all, and indeed from Cambridge in the 21st century.

There's ghost in my house

It was a sociable department and Chris and I were made welcome by, among others, Ralph Pickford and his wife Ruth, Robin Gilmour, and Peggy Emerson, who had done important work a few years previously with Rudolf Schaffer on infants' hierarchy of attachment figures (usually, though not invariably, with mum at the top). The ethos of the department was, however, ghostly. There was a pleasant Highlander who taught cognitive psychology, but he was out of the main stream in the department and had collected no data since his Ph.D.. Though clearly a highly intelligent man, he was coasting. There was a lively Englishman who taught visual perception and visual information processing, and he too did no research and lots of sailing on Loch Lomond. Just how isolated these two were was brought home to me in my first staff-meeting at which we discussed how the department would advertise for the next

Chair of Psychology to replace Ralph Pickford, who was retiring. The general tenor was that this was a department interested in *people*, in *the social context*. "We must make it plain," someone said, "that this department *is in the world*. Look what happened to Edinburgh: they appointed somebody working on ants' brains!" He was talking about David Vowles, some of whose work was indeed on insects, and some of whose lectures on physiological psychology I had attended at Oxford (the fact that, say, foraging ants can achieve hugely complex forms of spatial coding with primitive nervous systems, was surely not "in the world"). The vision guy did not like the way the discussion was going and ventured that, like it or not, one of the dominant currents in psychology these days was the study of information-processing. This roused to anger an otherwise timid young lecturer: "Oh that's just a *value judgement*!" Along with, "positivist," 'reductionist" and one or two others, this was the kind of language that built a firewall against realty in those days.

It may seem pointless and unseemly to dwell on the various ways that Glasgow was a poor department of psychology in those days. This poverty does, though, touch on the Ghost King. The ethos then was a mild form of what I described in the first part of the book: the assumption that psychology is the study not of the determinants of mentality but of its nature, in all its zoo-like variety. Anything gleaned about what humans do is grist to the mill. If the theoretical framework within which you do this gleaning (sorry, read and teach about other people's gleaning) is as unquestioning as religious faith well that simply does not matter.

As for the kind of research that was going on there in 1973, the profile was not all bad, but when it was bad it was, like the girl in the rhyme, horrid. As for the good, Steve Duck (whose view of the department I found meshed with mine just before we both left) was beginning his important work on long-term friendship formation, and this was to be continued in Lancaster and later in the USA.

Here are two examples of the bad, also examples of an almost childlike faith in Freud in one case and in Laing in the other. In my first few weeks I asked somebody what she was up to research-wise and she told me she was working on a "new" (many years old) version of the Rorschach (ink blot) Test. Second, the guy in the next office was a Laingian, who told me that Laing's book with David Cooper called *Reason and Violence* was not *supposed* to make sense. This did not stop him believing, however, that all schizophrenia was socially caused. He said that basically there were two kinds of theories of schizophrenia: "process" theories (social causation ones) and biological ones (he called them something else - forgotten). His aim was to *demonstrate* that all schizophrenia was of the process kind. I don't know how he pursued this research, in fact I saw little of him, despite the fact our office doors had windows in them. In fact he also told me that the way to give the impression that you were around and working even when you were, say, at home watching sport on the telly, was to leave a book on the desk. The book he chose for this was *The Divided Self.*

Now both of these people were admirable in their different ways. The first was kindly and serious-minded, if a little eccentric, and the second was intelligent, quick-witted and funny (his evidence against astrology was that Geminis were supposed to like velour, whereas he, as a Gemini, could "take it or leave it"). It was not a matter of being stupid or mendacious then: it was a matter of relaxing into a view of psychology in which you find a sympathetic of view of human mentality and set up house in it, avoiding the merest glance out of the window onto other prospects. And all the time the reader must bear in mind that I was hardly immune to this myself.

I only stayed in Glasgow for a year. This has always been a matter of huge regret to me as I loved the city — we both did — and have always felt (which I am) half-Scottish — "Aye, half Scotch, half water," as one of the removal men put it. One stimulus to the move away was nasty and embarrassing while the other was veering towards the rational.

From the Lüscher Colour Test to Tom Bower

The office I occupied (out in the farther reaches of the Adam Smith Building, well away from the main corridor of offices) had two desks in it, with the other one belonging to an Indian MA student whom I never saw. Assuming she had only been squatting in the office when it was empty, I thought she would never turn up and so I could use this largish room for testing children, with the plan being to try out my ideas for a nonverbal test of length conservation using a train-transfer design. This was my big project at the time. But turn up she did, frequently with her husband in tow; something that was disappointing. When I found that her MA research was on The Lüscher Colour Test my disappointment slithered down to despair. The Lüscher Colour Test makes the Rorschach ink-blot test look like The All Souls Fellowship examination. In this, the subject sets out some colour patches in order of preference, after which a personality profile is given based on these preferences. The evidence for its validity is that people tend to agree with these here profiles.

There is a technical term for tests like the Lüscher, and that is "a right load of nappy solution" (said in a Yorkshire accent). As it happens, Chris had once brought home a copy of it from Holborn Library in our London days, and this test soon came to feature in many a dinner-party aftermath. The book told my extravert, highly sociable, and energetic wife — she was later to become a Labour MP — that she should come out of her shell.

The problem with my plan to test children in the office was that the MA student was also a student of a Professor in Dehli who was a good friend of Ralph Pickford; and Ralph had more or less promised that she would be given a desk. This could have been sorted out in 10 minutes, and would have been by Arthur Summerfield. Instead, an extraordinary staff meeting was called. My line was that I saw no good reason why I, as a lecturer, should be sharing an office with an MA candidate and why I should not use my good-sized room for testing. While there are ways of making that point in a dignified and ameliorative way, the only social option available to me in real time was cold truculence. After a long academical argy-bargy it was agreed that the student would move out, with the cost to me being that I became about as popular as Banquo's ghost (in fact my Laingian next-door-neighbour made exactly this comparison). Was there a darker undercurrent? Maybe. In any event it played on my sleeping mind: "Oh come on now. Some of my best friends are racists," I dreamt I said to a table-full of my colleagues in the coffee room.

I didn't blame Ralph Pickford for this. He was a gentleman and belonged to a generation in which university teaching was a profession for gentlemen. Though I did of course blame myself in part for addressing the china shop head down. In fact, what I mostly blamed then, and what I blame now, was psychology itself. Do geography departments give desk-space to flat-earthers? Do astronomy departments appoint astrologers, and English departments illiterates? One thing I am trying to bring to life in this narrative is that some psychology had then — has *now* — a kind of built-in bullshit-compliance or acceptance frenzy. This psychology can be infinitely accommodating, because it knows that really there is nothing there, any more than there is something there beneath one of M. R. James's fluttering sheets on the Suffolk coast.[39] You try to see if colour preference predicts personality; it may come off, it may not; and whatever happens your "psychology" has been *done*. After all, you can't win 'em all.

The Lüscher colour test is *psychology* so, let her get on with her work. Yes and it's bullshit too. Oh that's just a value judgement. So is "Hitler was a bad man." You of all people

---

[39] His famous ghost story: "Listen and I'll come to you my lad."

should not bring Hitler into it! If you are not asking 5- year-olds trivial questions you're trying to expel those who just want to find something out about people … Where's your liberal-mindedness!

And so if you accept the *content* of loopy research you will also feel drawn to accepting whoever is doing it, accommodating them and accommodating *to* them.

Well that's the "nasty and embarrassing" reason out of the way. Before I get to the "veering-on-the-rational" one I need to touch on something in a more up-beat way. I'd told Peggy Emerson about my research plans (trying to show nonverbal competence in tasks like conservation in very young children), so she suggested that I go through to Edinburgh to see Tom Bower who had been doing something along these lines, not with children — with *babies*.

A word about Tom Bower. No decent history of developmental psychology could be written without giving Bower a Prince's role. Before Bower, developmentalists generally believed that Piaget had more or less said the last word on infant cognitive capacities, or rather the last sentence, which is, more-or-less: "These capacities develop late and depend upon the development of motor skill." I mean capacities such as depth perception; size constancy (things farther away look smaller while we know they're not); and, most notably, *object permanence* (our knowledge that objects continue to exist when we are not currently perceiving them). To put it crudely, the flaw in Piaget's way of thinking was that maybe he was finding that their development depended upon motor development because his method of assessing their abilities depended upon it.

What Bower did as early as the mid 1960s — I recall Nick Mackintosh telling us about the size constancy work in one of the prelim lectures — was to devise techniques that didn't depend upon such abilities as reaching and searching to assess babies' knowledge of objects. For example, they would be reinforced with a jolly peekaboo for turning their heads to a block 1 metre away. Would they generalise this response to the same block 3 metres away despite the fact that it now looked three times smaller? If they are 5 months old, yes they will (plus many control conditions of course).

Turning to object permanence, Piaget found that babies will not, until they are 8 months of age, search for objects that have become completely occluded, despite being able to search for them when they are partially occluded. Bower argued, however, that this may be due to the fact that they know that their, say, toy is still there behind the cushion, but they cannot, for whatever reason, organise the search for it. Accordingly, Bower arranged events that would be surprising to any baby who knew a thing was still there even if it was out of sight. The infant's surprise was measured by drop in heart-rate (which shows orienting to a stimulus). For example, a ball moves in from left to right and rolls behind a screen. The screen is then lifted and the ball is no longer there. A baby who thought the ball should still be there would show a drop in heart-rate, while a baby who thought that out of sight means out of existence would not. Babies of 20 weeks show appropriate surprise.

To put it mildly, it's not everybody who cares about this kind of thing. For anybody who does, however, Bower's genius is evident. What about conservation? The same logic can be applied. Indeed, at the conscious, verbal level children of 6 years may not know that weight is conserved through visual transformation: may not know, for example, that play-dough grows no heavier if you roll it into a ball. Perhaps they may appreciate this perfectly well on the level of action — on what Piaget called "the sensorimotor level." In fact, Bower had recently been collaborating with Pierre Mounoud from Geneva (Piaget's home university) on a study showing that 16-month-olds will use the same strength of hand-grip to pick up a block and the same arm-muscle tension to hold it steady when it is handed to them after the block has been visually transformed. This was a sensorimotor conservation of weight — as nonverbal as one could wish.

I recall driving into Edinburgh along Princess Street listening to the newly released *Killing me Softly with his Song* on the backseat transistor feeling childishly excited about meeting T. G. R. Bower, imagining him waiting behind a desk in a lab coat in something like a clinic. In fact it was more like going to score. When I eventually found Bower's quarters, which were in a backstage area behind a proscenium stage, I entered dimly lit rooms where Jimi Hendrix hung from the wall and played softly in the background. There was no Tom, but there was a pretty research assistant in floating clothes. Tom was at a wedding and would be along soon. The study being run that day was one on reaching in the dark. Bower had been finding that if the invisibility of the object is caused by turning off the room lights rather than by occluding the object with a screen or container babies are more likely to reach; which is consistent with his view that behind-occluder reaching is difficult, because young babies don't know what it means for two objects to occupy the same bit of space. In fact, the baby I saw, via infra-red illumination, did not so much reach as cry. And cry. I would not do any infancy research myself till 40 years later, when I learned to live within the element of crying.

Fed up with waiting I decided to cut my losses and head back to Glasgow —just as Tom Bower turned up. He was not, in the journalistic cliché, "tired and emotional" after a good wedding party, but he was certainly radically relaxed. After greeting me warmly and apologetically he fielded some telephone calls from the press about the groom ("Yes you can quote me. He was a very good bachelor") and took me upstairs to his office, where he dispensed just the kind of advice I needed and told me about his engagement with Piaget on his frequent trips to Geneva. This was fascinating stuff. Bower would present the old man – "Le Patron" as they called him — with his latest findings, findings that clearly challenged both his timetable for development and his way of assessing infants' abilities. Piaget would clamber slowly up to a high shelf to dig out some of his unpublished writings showing how he had either predicted, or prepared the conceptual ground for, these results.

In passing, I'll point out that certainly the Mounoud and Bower work on sensorimotor weight conservation, far from being a challenge to Piaget's thought, fell squarely within it. To explain, the essence of the theory is that knowledge of the basics like object permanence, space, time, and causality are "constructed" through the infant's own actions on the world before being re-acquired on the conceptual-linguistic plane many years later. For example, it will not be until children are around about 6 or 7 years that they can engage in "transitive reasoning" and conclude "Peter is taller than Paul" from "Peter is taller than John" and "John is taller than Paul." However, some time between 12 and 18 months babies can, as Piaget had demonstrated with his own three children (Jacqueline, Lauren and Lucienne), work out, for example, that a watch-chain is under a cushion, and search for it, having seen it being put under a beret and then a cushion put on top of the beret. In short, they know the transitive relationship of behind "on the sensorimotor level." Given this, the idea that infants can *act* on the basis of the conservation of length is as a thoroughly Piagetian result.

This Bower-hour was one of the best psychology hours I would spend; and I headed happily back to Glasgow. It is well known that things later went badly wrong in Bower's career. I won't presume to speculate on why, except to say that, as in the case of Laing, alcohol played a central role. Before things went wrong, however, he sparked the revolution in infancy research that was to sweep in from the USA in the mid 1980s. These later researchers adopted exactly the same logic as Bower —ask whether infants are surprised when they see an event that seems to violate a principle of which they seem to be ignorant — and even adopted some of his displays (Elizabeth Spelke did), with the only difference being that they used a different measure of surprise — looking-time (longer looking =

more surprise). Heart-rate drop is a crude measure and looking-time is a sensitive one. More on looking-time later, and on how it is the warp and weft of infancy research these days.

A BPS conference and "the a-theoretical papers that <u>pollute</u> this literature"

I was hoping to see Bower a few weeks later at the annual BPS (British Psychological Society) conference in Liverpool — which will bring me to my "veering-to-the-rational" reason for leaving Glasgow.

Developmentally, the line up of speakers was great: Richard Cromer, one of the world's leading developmental psycholinguists; Peter Smith on children's play; Tom Bower in a symposium with Peter Bryant as the discussant; and others. One of the others was new to me — a young and statuesque lady from Piaget's department in Geneva, called Olga Maratos, talking on imitation of facial gestures in babies. For Piaget, the ability to mirror the facial gesture of a model (like tongue protrusion or lip-pursing) cannot be an early accomplishment because it is the baby's developmental task to correlate what she sees another's face doing with what she feels she is doing with her own face. Indeed, how can she learn this *at all*, without arranging a mirror-selfie with the other? Piaget's rather implausible suggestion was that an auditory "index" is used. For example, the baby learns to mimic tongue protrusion via the raspberry sound index afforded when you poke your tongue out and blow.

Maratos reported a study showing that *neonates* will imitate facial gestures. While her study did not nail the matter down and involved little more than videotaping mother-baby interactions, it raised exciting nativist possibilities (yes I know: to apply "exciting" to babies poking their tongues out may simply show what a sheltered life some of us lead). In fact, this study was never published in a journal and only appeared in Maratos's Ph.D. in the same year. It was left to the American Andrew Meltzoff to nail the matter down, which he did brilliantly in his Ph.D. research at Oxford, published in *Science* four years later. In his study, he videotaped the neonates' faces when they were exposed to a number of facial gestures: tongue protrusion, lip pursing, and mouth widening. He then showed the videos to judges who had to decide whether a gesture was being presented and, if so, what it was. In a conversation many years later Andy described to me his trips to Geneva to tell Piaget about this work; and for this result there was no possibility of some earlier writings anticipating it. "How rude!" Piaget said when he heard about the neonatal tongue-poking. But he was and continued to be fascinated by the work and always wanted to hear the latest on it. He did not, as has become common,[40] look for methodological loopholes or reach

---

[40] I am thinking here of Moshe Anisfeld who has practically dedicated his career to scepticism: Anisfeld M. (2005) No compelling evidence to dispute Piaget's timetable of the development of representational imitation in infancy. In *Perspectives on imitation: from neuroscience to social science, vol. 2: Imitation, human development, and culture* (ed.s Hurley S., Chater N.). pp. 107–131. Cambridge, MA: MIT Press.

for the loopy notion that it was a sort of reflexive response adapted for feeding: he wanted to know more. This is not to say that Le Patron was ever the remotest bit happy about people *within* his institute running sceptical experiments, as Peter Bryant had found when he was a visitor there in the mid-Sixties. I guess he thought: "How rude!"

The symposium I had been looking forward to was the one with Tom Bower and Peter Bryant, and before that happened I went to the tail end of a symposium in which somebody called John Shotter was attracting most of the audience questions. What to say about Shotter? To somebody like me who thinks, given a nuance or two, that psychology that does not bite the scientific bullet is illusion and self-indulgence I ought not to approve of people like him who want to embed psychology deeply in social practice and well away from the laboratory. In fact, I have always had a warm regard for Shotter. Yes, there is something about the nexus of — here we go — ethnomethodogy, ethogenics, symbolic interactionism, Verstehen psychology, micro-sociology, social constructivism and the rest that can sets the teeth on edge, but there are reasons to like what Shotter was doing at the time and reasons to admire how he sticks to his guns. The main reason is that, in contrast to some of those who followed in his wake, he was driven by a Wittgenstinian-Vygotskian *enthusiasm* for a certain "image of man" (his phrase) not by contempt for the poor benighted plodders who adopt the scientific model, the kind of contempt that I saw in somebody I would later teach — who is to come. A minor reason is that Shotter is surely right that there is a naiveté in the standard laboratory social psychology experiment: your subjects' reactions are indeed embedded in their construction of the social set-up because the experiment is itself a social event. And on a personal level, I later got to know him a little and found him a likeable, highly-intelligent, and magnanimous man.

It might be said, though, that magnanimity was in rather short supply in the symposium I had driven all this way to witness. I sat near the back scanning the hall for Bower's shaggy head. Neither head nor body was there, because he'd missed the plane from Edinburgh. The unforgettable paper was one by J. G. Wallace from Warwick. Wallace had been collaborating on computer-models of children's performance on Piagetian tasks like conservation and class-inclusion with David Klahr from Carnegie-Mellon. In the class-inclusion experiment, children below 7 or so years give every impression of failing to understand the relation between the larger of two sub-classes and the total class, affirming, for example, that if there are 10 tulips in a bunch and 2 roses that there are more tulips than flowers altogether. Later work from the USA showed that children of about 8 or 9 years who correctly affirm that there are more flowers than tulips may change their minds if tulips keep being added. It's a striking phenomenon that Piaget plausibly explained, as he explained all these phenomena including conservation, in terms of children lacking mental flexibility. This is, when they attend to the larger sub-class their judgement is, as it were, glued there and cannot accommodate to the glaring fact that there can never be more (say) horses than animals altogether: a thought cannot be un-thought by young children because their perception-like minds lack reversibility (see p.60 above.). This kind of explanation is unsatisfying, however, in itself, because it is mere metaphor outside of Piagetian theory, while itself being stuck in the Piagetian hermeneutic circle. Accordingly, psychologists who had the skills to do so (often from an engineering background) turned to computational models in the interests of rigour and explicitness and in the hope that the models would make novel predictions.

As somebody once said, "in the early '70s even the cops had long hair and flared trousers" — I would add: "even Chomsky" — so Wallace was rather a striking figure with his militaristically shorn and suited demeanour. The guy next to me said, "Now there's a conformist," when Wallace walked up to the platform. He read his difficult and impressive paper with a similarly shorn and suited Scottish enunciation making few concessions to the audience, most of whose members were, I am sure, as dumfounded as I was. Though I recall from his comments afterwards that the Highland cognitive psychologist from Glasgow certainly got the message — a feat in itself.

Peter Bryant did his discussant's job with his usual benign humour and insight. When he got to Wallace's paper he began with (more or less): "Class inclusion ... Well, frankly, I wouldn't touch this task with a barge-pole. Dr Wallace has touched it with a [possibly a very mild expletive here like "ruddy" or "blinking"] great computer..." going on to say that class-inclusion failure is so labile a phenomenon that you can make it come and go by the way you emphasise the phrases in the instructions. He then made some criticisms of the model and waited for the dust to settle. Settle it did not. Wallace was furious and in his reply said more or less that at least he and Klahr could give an account of the mental processes that had not developed and were to develop, unlike, he said turning sharply to Peter, "those who write the a-theoretical papers that POLLUTE this literature." When I got back to our North Wales friends, who were putting me up, I related all this with great excitement, to such an extent that it may have seemed to them more a matter of "up with me."

I have to admit that I suffered from an animus against computational modelling — or more broadly the mentality-digital computer analogy — for the next 20 or so years and even tried to argue against it in my second book published in 1984. Now, however, I wish there were more of it, fearing that the lure of neuroimaging has made us think we stand less in need of a computational level, an explanatory level between the conscious and the neural.

The conference was a success and it left me with the impression that Liverpool must have a thriving psychology department. Indeed, I saw two impressive papers by members of the department in a symposium called Formal and Informal Systems in Psychology: one by Denis Bromley on informal systems, owing much to Stephen Toulmin (p.84 above), and another by Sandy Lovie on formal systems, owing much to Hullian drive theory (p.41). Added to this, the department was about to move into a spanking new building with labs and workshops, animal houses, and all the paraphernalia of a proper department of *experimental* psychology. So, when a lectureship came up there I applied.

I got the job (with a Ph.D., yes, though still with no publications, bar a Piaget-bashing piece in the *New Scientist*), and nearly failed to get it despite being the only person on the short list; for which I blame the fact that our North-Wales friends lived next door to a pub. It was the Manchester Poly interview all over again; but worse. They offered me the post after the interview — a long time after — and The Head of Department, Professor Leslie Hearnshaw, took me to lunch at Staff House. We sat at a long table with people from other departments and the upper administrative echelons and listened as somebody just down the table held forth about Psychology's interview debacle: they had only shortlisted one person and he had turned out to have "an appalling stammer." Not a good beginning then.

We left Glasgow early because Chris was pregnant with our daughter Charlotte and we had to get registered with the maternity backups soonest. I doubt very much whether anybody was disappointed by this early departure. When we were settling into our flat near Birkenhead in the late summer, a cheque for £5.25 arrived from the Glasgow department. This fine sum was my leaving present, collected from staff donations. What a pity, the accompanying note had said, that I could not have been there for a proper farewell and speeches — speeches, which, if sincere, would have included the phrases "good riddance" and "It's Scotland's oil."

Carl Jung once dreamt that Liverpool was the pool of life; and he was wrong

The Liverpool staff could not be faulted for academic rigour, intelligence, attention to detail, and good teaching. While there was humour too, and some kindliness, for me the place had an arctic feel to it — a place where such positives seemed to have been generated by a deterministic, impersonal mechanism. It did not help that I lived in Chester after the initial few months and was equally detached as a social being even when I was at work.

They had indeed moved to a new building, and their colour was an appropriate ice-green — to the pillar-box red of Sociology and the buff of Economics. There were acres of mechanical and electrical workshop, never utilized, and skiving, satirical technicians with time on their hands for plenty of "foreigner" jobs to earn a bit extra. "I don't see why we shouldn't work at home," Brian the chief technician once said to me, "You lot do."

Well what, you may ask, has all this to do with my sheep-from-goats-in-psychology project? Only to make the rather obvious point that while there may be rigour and all the other handmaidens of experimental psychology, without some intellectual heat you will not only fall short, but turn people off. Experimental psychology, unless it is something that you care about with some urgency rather than as something to get over to undergraduates, can indeed be cold and low-pressure.

One person who stood out as evidence against my charmless negativity was Graham Wagstaff, a social psychologist, who also joined the department with me in 1973. He was a brilliantly engaging lecturer and nobody could accuse him of owning no intellectual passions. One of these was showing that hypnosis is not a trance state, but more like a state of social compliance-cum-licence (and I'm the last person to criticise a negative motivation). Other warm interests of his were the psychology of political orientation — back to the Authoritarian Personality (p.66) — and psychoanalysis. As for the latter, year-after-year in his practical classes he would find a correlation between being high on "the anal triad" of parsimony, stubbornness and tidiness, and preferring drawings of big over small bums. "Explain it?" as John Laurie used to say at the end of his TV ghost stories: "*Ye cannae!*"

Graham and I published an empirical paper together on astrology,[41] critical of an earlier study on which Hans Eysenck's (p.47) name had appeared as co-author, showing that Air and Water signs are more extravert than Earth and Fire signs and that Water signs are relatively neurotic. We found that when the subjects are ignorant of the purpose of the study, and when you look at Moon and planet positions too (of

---

[41]   Russell, J. & Wagstaff, G. F. (1983) Extroversion, neuroticism, and time of birth. *British Journal of Social Psychology, 22*, 27-32.

course, people tend to be ignorant of these) the effect vanishes. I have to admit to having had a perverse desire for us to replicate the effect.

Leslie Hearnshaw only had a couple of years to go before he retired, and when he retired his loss was sorely felt. It was felt on the social level, because he had an aura of quiet dignity that discouraged self-interested and cheap remarks; and when he left there were many of those to be heard in staff meetings. His loss was felt in teaching, because he taught two fine courses, one on the history of psychology and one called Fundamental Problems in Psychology (a philosophical course essentially). I was going to take these over when he left and so I attended them. This from a lecture by Leslie on behaviourism, will remain indelibly in my mind. He was discussing Ryle's *The Concept of Mind* and Ryle's idea that really our psychology is fairly transparent to us, that rather little stands in need of explanation. His repudiation of this was simple. He undid and quickly did up a button of his waistcoat and declared: "That I can do this is an *absolute miracle*. And of course it needs explaining." Exactly.

Leslie was the official biographer of Cyril Burt — the "old delinquent" touched on earlier. His biography, as beautifully-written as was all his work, came to the nuanced and reluctant conclusion that Burt did indeed invent data showing a high correlation between the IQs of identical twins reared apart. I saw him give a plenary presentation on his book at the Annual BPS conference in Aberdeen in '79 or so; and he did so to great acclaim, seeking to excuse Burt's fraudulence in clinical terms. Indeed, the address was masterly and received a standing ovation. When the applause died down, a Liverpool colleague sitting next to me muttered, "Well he never did much when he was at Liverpool." This remark typified the department at its worse: mean spirited and mistrustful of any success that was not strictly local.

I was delighted to take on Leslie's courses, which I amalgamated into one long course called "History and Philosophy of Psychology," because I felt myself turning away from experimental psychology and towards more theoretical pursuits. I also found I enjoyed writing, and thought a book might materialise from all the reading I would have to do to teach it. While keeping a toehold in experimental child psychology, I associated scientific psychology with the icy stuff my colleagues researched and taught. I did not give a damn about measuring the toxicity of drugs, nor, I am ashamed to say, about memory deficits in the elderly. In short, I was being turned off by what I saw as the dreary, low-key empirical ethos at Liverpool. Yes, I bet a few of them could say a few choice things about me in return, the least of which would be that I had a weakness for what they would have called "soft" psychology — something with more than a little overlap with my king-of-the-ghosts psychology. Ironies aplenty here.

Right on – on write-off?

There was another way in which the Liverpool ethos could "turn people off" experimental psychology. I mean undergraduates this time, and the kind of radical student who flourished in the 1970s. I did say earlier that I would avoid even judicious use of the internet and indeed avoid researching the background to this narrative; but in the case of one I shall call Peregrine Trotter[*] I simply could not resist. This is a paraphrase of his Wikipedia page, written, I bet, by himself: "...then on to a degree in Psychology at the University of Liverpool in 1974 where he became involved in the radical politics of the city and found himself reacting against the traditional empirical psychology that was the bedrock of the Liverpool degree at the time. He read the work of John Shotter..." What marked out Peregrine and his friends for me was their pose of leftier-than-thou intellectual superiority. Indeed, it was common in those days to despise experimental psychology because it was not politically engaged or relevant; and this was hardly unique to Liverpool. A friend of ours from the Chester Labour Party referred to the Professor of Psychology who taught her visual perception at Keele University as "a lemon" because he would be describing the Müller-Leyer Illusion when there as a lot of, like, really radical stuff going on around the campus.

Staying in the political domain for one moment, I enjoyed provoking them in my lectures on social class and cognitive development. Within the ideology of Perry and his friends one should never talk about a social class being "cognitively disadvantaged," because that was to patronise them. Instead they preferred to patronise the denizens of Liverpool 8 by saying that "ripping off cars" — this was shouted out in a lecture — was their way of adapting to their environment; just as middle-class kids adapt to theirs. I pointed out that middle class kids can have a glass of wine on the lawn *and* rip off cars if the mood takes them. The Liverpool 8 inhabitants can only do one of these.

Meanwhile, Perry and Co. hunted round for some "radical critique" of psychological practice as the objective correlative of their frustration. There were plenty around, ranging from the good to the bad to the ugly. In any event, Peregrine Trotter has gone on to enjoy quite a successful career in the research area of how-people-talk-about-stuff.

Is this within the ghost-psychology cross-hairs? I mean what I called before the "ethnomethodogy, ethogenics, symbolic interactionism, Verstehen psychology, micro-sociology, social-constructivism" nexus. In a way it is and in a way it's not. When it comes to this kind of thing I am, as Norman Mailer described himself, a "left-conservative." When asked what he meant by this Mailer said, "If somebody tells me he has three trees and three men, that he has to destroy either the men or the trees, and asks me to decide which he should destroy, I will say, 'Let me see them'." In other words, while inclined to prefer experimental psychology and cognitive science to whatever socio-relativistic essence lies at the intersect of these approaches (I prefer people to trees), some of the writers in this area are a useful corrective, and have interesting things to say of a broadly Wittgenstinian kind. Certainly, John Shotter's

Images of Man in Psychological Research was both timely and has stood the test of time; Kenneth Gergen on the fluidity and historical relativism of self and social process tells us exactly why social psychology cannot be scientific in the way some would like it to be; while the work of the philosopher Rom Harré (the founding father of a form of "critical" psychology) is impossible to dismiss. And certainly too, if you read the work of some those who have set up camp in the territory that people like these have cleared for use, you will find something pretentious, boring, pointless, unimaginative, undemanding, and soppy-stern.

Let me illustrate this by contrasting Harré with the latter category in order to nail the ghostly nature of setters-up of camps. Consider first a position articulated both by Harré and by Shotter: the idea that psychological categories such as intentional versus unintentional are "socially constructed." Those who argue like this generally borrow Wittgenstein's thought that the language for so-called private mental episodes, like that of being in pain, is grounded not in the act of introspection onto some phenomenal something ("a beetle in the box"): it is grounded in overt social practice — pain behaviours and the like. The same idea can be extended to belief and desire. As Adam Morton argued,[42] rather than the meaning of what agents think and want being fixed by their, as it were, looking into their hearts, it is fixed by kind of public "theory" of how beliefs and desires function in the behavioural economy ("he expected there was beer in the fridge and that's

---

[42] In his book *Frames of Mind* 1968

why he's annoyed"). Morton called the idea that our understanding of mental state terms is analogous to a scientific theory "the theory theory;" and more of this much later. Given this, how do we explain the development of children's ability to judge when their own actions are *meant* or not? If they do not do so by accessing some private feeling of "meaning to do X" then maybe they do so by noticing how other people treat their (the child's) actions — as intentional or not. They get the category via social learning.

When Harré came to Liverpool to give a seminar on this topic, arguing more or less as I have just outlined, I asked a question (not something I did often) along the following lines: If a child comes to recognise her own action as intentional because of the way her parents treat it, then, for this to work, will she need some prior understanding of what *treating as-intentional* looks like? And to have *this* won't prior knowledge of the category "intentional" be necessary? His answer was that this social learning experience is a gradual ratcheting-up process, not the kind of one-off insight I described. I don't want to dwell on the issue of who is right in this kind of debate. My point is only that this *is* a worthwhile debate. There can be some to-and-fro about whether Wittgenstein was right to argue as he did and, if he was right, whether Harré-Shotter should apply this philosophical view in this empirical way. And, of course, one can argue about the evidence for the view and about the relevance of the fact that we now know, via the work of Tomasello, Gergely, Csibra and others,[43] that babies and toddlers are tremendously good at recognising intentional acts in others. The debate is viable because it is about social experience as *determinant*. It is psychology.

Now consider the camp-setter-upper way of being a student of social processes. This time, the topic is not the social as a determinant. It is just, well ... the social. How do we do things socially, together? Let's have a look at that. Let's have a look at how we use language and let's line up behind Ryle and Wittgenstein for good measure. Let's call this "discursive psychology." Yes, we are historically in Liverpool in the mid 1970s, but about that time you could not move for seedbeds for this kind of thing. Its full flowering we will deal with much later — with that and "phenomenological psychology." But to anticipate the flower, under the discursive approach to psychology one will do such things as look at how we "organise descriptions to manage our own accountability and that of others," look at ways in which people use psychological concepts "to do what they are doing," look at how people "negotiate their identity" through conversation. The empirical face of this? Looking at doctor-patient and counsellor-client interactions, at how "meanings" are managed when unhappy children ring *Child-Line* and when racists speak out.

---

[43]   Carpenter, M., Akhtar, N. & Tomasello M. (1998) 14 to 28 month old infants differentially imitate intentional and accidental actions. *Infant Behaviour and Development, 21,* 315-330. Also see: Yoon, Johnson and Csibra (2008) Communication-induced memory biases in preverbal infants. *Proceedings of the National Academy of Sciences of the United States of America,* 105, 13690-13695

This falls squarely within king-of-the-ghosts psychology, for these familiar reasons: not only it is just sterile journalism, but it's ego-inflation from the rabbit mind to the King of the Ghosts. The former (sterile journalism) may or may not speak for itself. As for the latter, the point is that the practitioners are quite happy to give the impression that in, say, looking at how a GP and a patient "negotiate meanings" around the patient's hypertension they are doing a kind of psychology that, oh how unlike all this laboratory stuff, not only tells us about how the mental is manifest in the social, but shows us how radically and provocatively refreshing are the people who do this kind of thing. When really it is just talking loosely (and wrongheadedly: are meanings being negotiated here?) about what we are sometimes like and sometimes tend to do.

Meanwhile, back in the historical narrative, I have to say that there was also something refreshing in the social-constructivist-Marxist-Leninist-you-name-it faction. They were mainly nice people, especially a Dr-Who-like Trotter-ally whose spelling was even worse than mine ("resurch" anyone?). Also, they were hard workers who did write essays that were to-the-point. Once one of them did not and produced a jargon-ridden rant. Recalling one of our 6th-Form routines I simply wrote at the end: "Every little breeze seems to whisper Peter Frank Cornwall Smith" and waited for the protest that never came.

Yes, it was irritating to read feedback comments on my colleague Ann Davies' excellent introductory course, like: "just a bourgeois talking shop " — though little more than that. The only people I disliked actually teaching were postgraduates taking the Diploma in Clinical Psychology. Their room was a floor up from mine and once entered it was like entering a hostile neighbour's sitting room. One afternoon I swore badly at a couple of young women who were passing notes and giggling during my halting address. Why should Teddy Smaile have all the best tunes?

Hello and goodbye to Keith; language development

Into this mix of frustration and improvised accommodations came my old Oxford friend Keith Stenning, having recently completed a Ph.D. in psycholinguistics with George Miller at the Rockerfeller Institute in New York. I thought this would mean things picking up on the intellectual and social fronts. In a way they did, but there was also some "picking down" and a weakening of our friendship. Keith and his first wife Paula stayed with us in Chester until they bought a place in Liverpool. I inflicted my commute on him. Perhaps the problem was that each of us classified the other as a Liverpool colleague. In any event, Keith didn't stay long, leaving what he called "the snake pit" for a Lectureship in Edinburgh a few years later. And for readers who know anything about the psychology of reasoning I can add: "and the rest is history." Keith has had a brilliant career.

   In those days, Keith and I had rather little in common intellectually. For it was a long time before I would become an advocate of the Chomskyan view of syntax and its development; and Keith was formalist through and through. I saw myself as a "functionalist" in those days. This can mean a number of things, and in the field of language development it meant explaining children's early ability to make well-formed utterances in terms of communicative intentions, in terms of the jobs that language could do for them (draw attention, get "goods and services," and so forth). It meant being distrustful of the very idea of innate preparedness for language while being very friendly towards the idea of social preparedness; and ultimately it meant the wild-goose project of reducing the complex machinery of syntax to acts of social meaning. No doubt when Peregrine Trotter and his friends heard me lecture on language development they though I was ripe for "turning," as they indeed attempted.

It's interesting — though hardly interesting *sub specie aeternitatis* — that the intellectual trajectories of Keith and I crossed, at least with regard to grammar development, so that each of us now holds the position the other used to hold. Whereas Keith now thinks that Michael Tomasello and others are right that language acquisition is grounded in joint attention and other kinds of social processes and strategies, I think that we are born with cognitive machinery dedicated to learning the syntax of language, and that a child might jointly attend and exercise a theory of other minds till she is blue in the face, but will never learn syntax without it.

Anyway, when we meet post-Liverpool we remain on shared, not disputed, territory. One of the most pleasant post-Liverpool re-encounters with Keith was at my son Paddy's stag night in Edinburgh a few years ago. It was just like being back at Oxford where as the beer flowed Keith discoursed — this time on Phil Johnson-Laird's shortcomings as a logician (he says) and on the tar-baby of the Wason Selection Task.[44]

One of the things that triggered my move towards a nativist view of language development and away from a empiricist view that parents, as it were, take a child's hand and lead her into language was the birth of our daughter Charlotte in 1973. Chomsky talks about the "stimulus" to grammar development as being too "impoverished" to support its learning, by which he means that the sentences a child hears do not wear their structures on their sleeves and that the child needs innate appreciation of the latent structures if she is to unearth them. This is his famously Platonic "poverty of the stimulus argument." Well, I certainly thought the linguistic input to Charlotte was hardly designed for learning: it was impoverished in a more mundane way. Yes, we directed speech at her, often in the form of bizarre questions ("So you're dressed as a *Peugeot* mechanic today then!") and we answered her questions; but there was no sense in which we tutored her in language. She watched us speak, and heard lots of "little local difficulty" utterances, adult narratives, and private jokes; then she just started speaking. And it was like a miracle. Not the least of the miracle was her passion to relate experiences, with little or no grasp of word-order, at around 18 months to an ignorant audience. On a trip to Chester Zoo with my mother and Christine she saw some leopard cubs being fed, and on returning said to me said, "Lep-cubs, foody, gramma."

---

[44]   This is an hypothesis-testing task that 80% of undergraduates fail. It will crop up again in the Question Time section.

Creeping up on the hard problems with Ray and Howard

After the departure of Keith I had nobody to discuss psychology with — disagreeing didn't matter; at least it was a discussion — let alone to have lunch with. The former problem was solved by somebody who was at that time a Reader in Geriatric medicine — one Raymond Tallis (though the lunch problem went unsolved). Ray, as he was known to us, is now a big name; and this was a long time ago — around 1982. This came about because, in those days, the psychology of ageing was the department's foremost interest. We were interviewing a candidate for a lectureship in this area, and Ray was co-opted as a member of the panel. I was on the panel too. The post-interview discussion was a bit stormy, because I did all I could to prevent Denis Bromley, our head of department, from appointing somebody I thought was hopeless. This may have given Ray the false belief that I was feisty, or it may have been because he'd heard I was interested in philosophical psychology; or both. In any event, he asked me to join a philosophy-psychology discussion group he was setting up with somebody from the philosophy department — Howard Robinson.

This was tremendous. At last life felt like the life of an academic. Ray and Howard were different kinds of intellect (Ray discursive-fleshy, Howard analytical-skeletal) — yet both shared an affability which, in those days at least, Howard would have put down to their both having the Sun in Libra (apparently, I only have the Moon in Libra — another falling short). It seemed to me then that Ray was marked out for the future fame he achieved as what might be called a pamphleteer against the self-overreaching of the biological sciences. If you hear the terms "Darwinitis" or "Neuromania" these days then it's probably Ray saying them; and this was the tune Ray sang in the 1980s too. I agreed with him, while thinking that he was essentially doing no more than re-stating the problem — I mean *The* Problem: the mind-body problem. Whatever his position on the various things we three read and wrote for these meetings, what was impressive about Ray was his energy and good humour. He had a demanding clinical post and yet wrote and read something serious in a literary or philosophical vein every evening, usually refreshed by those plastic flagons of weak beer you could buy in those days (Howard and I were the more determined red-wine guzzlers at the meetings). Some evenings he would do a reading of his poems in a pub.

Howard, now at the University of Central Europe in Budapest, had transported an Oxford island to within a stone's throw of Strawberry Fields. He maintained a flat in Oxford, and evoked Oxford in his manner, thought, and speech — which I found a delight (echoes of *"Well he would, wouldn't he"*?). Howard was a Berkeleyan Idealist, which means he agreed with Bishop George Berkeley that to believe in the mind-independent existence of a material world is tantamount to atheism; and in early meetings he shared with us drafts of his influential book *Matter and Sense: a Critique of Contemporary Materialism* (1982). In passing, Howard was much influenced by Rom Harré's (p.122) book *Causal Powers* when writing his own book. We have no knowledge of a material world, this view runs, only of a phenomenal world of sensation. What causes these sensations, if not matter? They are underpinned divinely. Of course, I had my turns at trying to "refute it *thus:*"[45] ... err ... the world can also put an end to sensation, a.k.a. kill us; while Ray's attempts to resist this view were more fluent and complex.

At this point I shall, with both hands waving free, say a few things about the mind-body problem and how it relates to scientific psychology. The problem is that there seem to be two kinds of entity: the world of experience (pains, joy, colours, sneaking suspicions about Dr. Loomis's motivation) and the world of material stuff (nuts, bolts, moussaka, not to mention that stuff inside our heads roughly the colour of moussaka). And it seems that the external, material stuff causes our sensations, but may not (dreams and so forth). So we seem to be stuck with two kinds of entity, with the question then being "How are the two related?" To my mind the only honest answer to this is, as the Irish say, "I haven't got a baldy!" The point of philosophy is to speak up and think up, no matter how implausible the position. Here are some meaty implausibles:

1. Howard's position — Idealism. This does logically solve the problem while doing so at the cost of making the mind-independence/objectivity of the external world divine. But who is to say that God exists? Or is the existence of consciousness a kind of consideration in favour of God's existence? Some would argue that.

---

[45] Dr Johnson "refuted" it by kicking a stone and saying "I refute it *thus*."

2. Behaviourism[46] deconstructs phenomenal experience into: (a) mere informational access to the physical; and (b) to *talk* about subjective states, grounded in social practice in a Wittgenstinian manner described in earlier passages (Howard once said to us: "Wittgenstein never opened his mouth but to utter a falsehood;" while the man himself unhelpfully said that the mental is "not a something but not a nothing either"). Well, you just try maintaining a belief in the unreality of the mental, as its being just verbal routines and perceptual access, for more than a minute or two.

3. Panpsychism. This is a new kid on the block, the progeny of Galen Strawson. The claim is that matter is actually conscious. The brain, most centrally, is conscious matter. This gives physics rather than psychology the task of explaining how matter can be conscious. Colin McGinn writes: "Panpsychism is surely one of the loveliest and most tempting views of reality ever devised; and it is not without respectable motivations either. There are good arguments for it, and it would be wonderful if it were true — theoretically, aesthetically, humanly. Any reflective person must feel the pull of panpsychism once in a while. The trouble is that it's a complete myth, a comforting piece of balderdash. Sorry Galen, I'm just not down with it (and isn't there something vaguely hippyish, i.e., stoned,

---

[46] Perhaps Daniel Dennett is the best spokesman for this kind of view.

about the doctrine?)," [47] and many us "feel the pull" of the McGinn dismissal.

4. Functionalism has much in common with behaviourism, with the clear difference being that the former takes the mind to be a representing device through-and-through, not just a device for responding to stimuli and generating behaviour, verbal or otherwise. On functionalism, mental states are like the states of a digital computer: caused by inputs, causing outputs, and having internal causal connectedness with one another. It is like saying: "Just look how much mentalising can be done without any phenomenal states. Isn't that enough for you!" And this is tantamount to wishing the problem away.

5. Dualism (mind and body are two different "substances"). Well yes they do seem like that; and that is merely to state the problem. How do they causally interact then? Does it make any sense at all to say that they do?

6. Monism (mind and body are a single entity). Whatever variety of monism you adopt it feels either false or banal. False, because experience and the physical are so *different*; and not just in the way that water and H_2O are different. While, yes of course, they are one thing — a brain thing — but that, as in dualism, is just to restate the problem.

---

[47] Colin McGinn 'Hard Questions' in *Consciousness and Its Place in Nature: Does Physicalism Entail Panpsychism?*, ed. by Galen Strawson (Exeter: Imprint Academic, 2006), p.93.

Now, what seems to emerge from the above —this was and is Ray's *Leitmotif*—is that no amount of knowledge about the brain is going to solve this problem; and that there is a kind of ego-inflation abroad, not among practising neuroscientists so much as among people who earn their living writing books on neuroscience, which fuels the view that the brain sciences are working steadily towards a solution to the mind-body problem. The latter — the brain journalists — seem to be in a permanent state of amazement that mental states line up with activity in fMRI-scanned-brains. Now the following is what would be truly amazing: that they did *not* line up; that brain states and conscious states varied independently.

None of this is to deny that psychologists can say a lot of interesting and true things about consciousness. It's the *relation* to brain states that stumps us. Consciousness received little mention in the undergraduate course at Liverpool; and this just put us in step with other departments of that time. Nowadays it gets more of a look-in, mainly because so much interesting work on attention and vision (see p.43 on blindsight) has emerged. For my money, the best book on consciousness around is one written by Jeffrey Gray (p.47) shortly before he died: *Consciousness: Creeping up on the Hard Problem*. And this is despite the fact that as you creep up, it creeps away.

The group continued beyond my departure from Liverpool in 1987, with the happy additions (before my departure) of Richard Latto, a one-time collaborator of Alan Cowey and yet a determined sceptic about blindsight, and of Richard Benthall, to drop yet another proto-famous name (I did warn about the slightly Zelig-aspect of all this); with the philosopher Mark

Sacks being an occasional contributor. I lost touch with Howard, having glimpsed him from a bus in the Oxford bus station in 2004 (said Mr Pooter). I attended a lecture Ray gave in 2008, going on to a dinner that Tony Marcel[48] had arranged for the purpose of introducing Ray to Jonathan Miller (no, neither the Dalai Lama nor Mick Jagger was present at this). It was interesting to see Ray again, a seeing that brought home to me that fact that personalities as well as joints and blood vessels harden with age. I can't say I took to the fedora; and was that a groupie! My admiration for him was, though, intact though hardened to the extent that I would add to the Ray-rundown of "doctor, philosopher, poet, novelist, literary critic and campaigner" … "compulsive writer of books with titles like *Reflections of a Metaphysical Flâneur*."

Baldwin and genetic epistemology

At this point I feel twinges of guilt about how I've presented the Liverpool department. It can't be denied that I received much support and encouragement from Denis Bromley, who succeeded Leslie Hearnshaw as head of department. That I would have sometimes have welcomed the firm smack of an Arthur Summerfield may be *my* problem. Denis was, as was Ralph Pickford in Glasgow, a humane man who always sought compromise. And like Ralph too, he tried to resolve disputes by

---

[48] Somebody who has made very significant contributions to the study of consciousness and who is also known for an occasional interesting turbulence.

calling extraordinary staff meetings. At one such we had to watch as the computer-officer/statistics teacher and a collaborator of Richard Latto had a heated dispute about some statistics question that I don't care to recall. In the words of Ann Davies it was like watching fighting cocks.

Denis, as a theoretical psychologist himself, encouraged me to write books and non-empirical journal papers, some of which grew out of the History and Philosophy course I was teaching. One of my lectures was on behaviourism, and thinking about this in terms of what it denied (representational states most broadly and what I called "acting from knowledge") I published a trilogy of papers in the journal *Behaviourism* on what kind of behaviour rats *would* have to evince to be said to act from knowledge and on what aspects of human behaviour can be said to depend on non-epistemic conditioning. I ended with the Baron de Charlus in a coda I was rather proud of, touching on Beckett's little book on Proust via the role of *habit* in the novel … Oh it was like 1965 all over again; except not remotely (I was helped somewhat in this by two animal-learning colleagues, Andrew Goudie and Ev Thornton. Andrew's name should have been on one of these three papers; but it just did not occur to me).

Then, more centrally, in researching the early influences on Piaget for a historical lecture I read James Mark Baldwin, an American philosopher-psychologist variously allied with some of the pragmatists and neo-Hegelians who were around in turn-of-the-century America. Baldwin was a mind-bogglingly energetic researcher on all kinds of things (colour vision in the African grey parrot springs to mind) and a writer on all kinds of things including mental development and evolution. Also, compellingly, he was somebody whose career ended early and in disgrace. Having been arrested in a raid on a "negro brothel" in Baltimore — he said it was the result of a student prank — his resignation from Johns Hopkins University was inevitable and eventually he left for Paris, where he met Piaget. Piaget said of Baldwin that he gave the impression of knowing a lot of facts about child development, while he did not see fit to mention them. This was what was so strange and perversely attractive — I mean to somebody who fancied he belonged in the intersect between psychology and philosophy — about Baldwin. He wrote an *a priorish* cognitive development in which the reader was assumed to know pretty well what children were like and what they could do while he alternately analysed and rhapsodized from first principles, from philosophical assumptions about the nature of knowledge and what you needed or had to do to acquire it.

Most people know what Piaget took from Baldwin; and it has to be said that this was fairly superficial and mainly on the level of terminology: the terms "assimilation" "accommodation," "circular reaction" (actions a baby can repeat at will), "schema," "genetic epistemology," and a few others. In any case, it was the difference between the two thinkers that interested me, especially as somebody highly sympathetic to what I have called "the Wittgenstein-Vygotsky axis" (p.58 above). Baldwin held the view that knowledge or meaning, as it were, "in" one mind must potentially be in other minds too, potentially to the knower/meaner. Having adopted the Kantian view that objective experience implies a correlative awareness of oneself as a knower (Kant's "the I-think that must accompany all my presentations"), Baldwin went beyond this principle to claim that there must be a corresponding awareness of these meanings or that piece of knowledge as being held in common. This was nothing if not a Wittgenstinian thought, and more immediately it will ring a bell with contemporary developmentalists who appreciate the importance of "joint attention," wherein children do not just happen to share attention to objects with other people, but are clearly aware of this fact by checking the other's attention. This is at once a kind of royal road to what another is experiencing and to the very idea that any knowledge worthy of the name is potentially public. It may also evoke the so-called "pedagogical stance" of Gergely and Csibra[49] — an innate predisposition to take adults to be people who point out to you, not mere episodic, local, and individual facts but general, shared, generic, public facts. Thus, if mother says "cat" when an animal appears the child takes this to be people's word for a kind of animal, not something that mum happened to call the animal at that time. Baldwin loved to invent terminology, with the earliest grasp of the commonness of meaning being called "syndoxic" (child sees commonness as a contingent fact) and a later one being called "synomic" (child see commonness as a kind of necessity).

At this point I can feel my nose rubbing in the fact that, while finding social constructivism (then and now) an unattractive doctrine, I thrilled to the sound of passages like

---

[49] G. Csibra and G. Gergely (2009) Natural pedagogy. *Trends in Cognitive Science, 13*, 248-153.

this one in Baldwin: "So of knowledge. *It is not a private possession; it is public property*. It begins common, stays common, claims to be common, enforces its commonness. No knowledge confined in one head, repeated in other private heads an infinity of times, would ever become an organic system of common knowledge...*The private thought is not an organic unit, it is a cognitive outcome*" (original emphasis, 1908, p.105). The seeming contradiction is easily resolved. Baldwin is saying: Here is a *social condition* on objective knowledge. By contrast, social constructivists are either saying: (a) psychological categories are socially, not biologically, determined; or (b) that the fluid social process within which meanings are socially negotiated (are they?) is a suitable object of study in itself. Yes, though Baldwin was given more to assertion than to argument, he did have a philosophical position that falls in line with Wittgenstein's. Though one can imagine Wittgenstein being outraged by his way of doing things.

And what a way that was. As I put it in the book I wrote comparing Baldwin and Piaget — *The Acquisition of Knowledge* (1978), the kind of title you might find on a wizard's bookshelf — "*Thought and Things* is difficult reading: new terms appear, reappear and generate others, abstractions breed abstractions and disappear into the shadows. But, as W. B. Yeats wrote of a work, which is almost comparable in that respect (Blake's *Jerusalem*), there is despite it all a 'mumbling wisdom'" (1978, p. 53). The problem is of course that it's hard to hear the mumbling wisdom above the cataract of obfuscating semantics and late-Jamesian syntax. I loved it though.

David Hamlyn (p.88), by now Professor of Philosophy at Birkbeck, was tremendously helpful to me when I was writing this book, sending me meticulous long-hand letters about where I was going right or wrong. During the writing I also put myself in touch with Wolf Mays, a philosopher at Manchester, who had worked with Piaget — I am still vague about what "worked" meant exactly— and who had one or twenty-two things to say about Piaget's "genetic epistemology" (more of which later). Colin McGinn's[50] memoir gives a fine character sketch of Wolf, to which I will not add, except to say that with me he alternated between being warmly supportive and terminally tetchy. His dismissals of certain famous philosophers were hilarious; though he did just about concede that Chomsky was "quite intelligent." Physically, he reminded me of Jiminy Cricket, and intellectually of nobody — a one-off.

Just after my book's publication Wolf organised a one-day conference in Manchester, one Saturday morning, on Piaget's genetic epistemology. He invited me to speak, along with David Hamlyn, Andy Young (then a developmentalist from Lancaster, now a cognitive neuropsychologist), a young philosopher from the LSE, and Wolf himself.

Another word in passing about genetic epistemology. For Piaget it meant that traditional questions about human knowledge could not merely be illuminated by reference to the growth of knowledge in children and to human evolution: they had to be addressed this way. To the traditionalist, this meant a

---

[50] *The Making of a Philosopher: My Journey Through Twentieth-Century Philosophy*

fatal blending of the empirical with the philosophical. David Hamlyn rather tended towards the traditional view, preferring to take genetic epistemology to mean the philosophical study of how knowledge acquisition is possible, a concern that goes back to Aristotle.[51] My position was this:[52] when philosophers discuss knowledge and the mind they do so from "platforms of empirical consensus," meaning a set of agreed facts about human life (e.g., tripping over is unintentional, while reaching for a glass is intentional). If we include facts about mental development these platforms change and so consequently will the philosophy also change (the same might be said of cognitive neuroscience). This position now reminds me of so-called "empirical philosophy" wherein finely-honed questionnaires determine just how many people share philosophical intuitions with philosophers (fewer than you would think).

Yes we do indeed regard "reaching for a glass" as intentional and claim responsibility for doing it, so I only had myself to blame for the Guinness-imbibing on the Friday night that guaranteed a disastrous talk the next morning in Manchester. In fact, when it comes to the link between drinking and car-crash public speaking I remind myself of the time when mankind had yet to sort out the causal linkage between sex and pregnancy. What's more, without fully realising it, I had gone back to my Glasgow strategy of seeking a relaxed public demeanour by way of not bothering: not only not seeming to bother, but not

---

[51]   D. W. Hamlyn (1976) Aristotelian epagoge. *Phronesis, 21*.

[52]   Argued in Russell, J. (1979) The status of genetic epistemology. *Journal for the Theory of Social Behaviour, 9*, 53-71.

actually *bothering*. I wrote my talk quickly in scruffy long-hand after dinner at my parent's house in Bristol, a talk that did not so much end as fade away. I never edited it. On that Saturday morning I felt after half a tortuous hour that I and the audience had had enough, so I just stopped. "That's it!" Coffee was early; and I stood in the queue making awkward small-talk with David Hamlyn.

I have to add in all fairness to the much-bad-mouthed-by-me Liverpool socio-Leninist-constructivist faction that many of them attended. They were engaged. Give them that. They were enthusiasts.

Inside the cognitive-developmental tent; hard rain in Geneva

Deriding something as "ghost psychology" does not hold me back from deriding quite a lot of flesh-and-blood psychology too, particularly of the developmental variety. I'm an equal-opportunities derider.

What I am considering now is the state of cognitive developmental psychology in the mid-'70s to early-'80s. It was dull to those inside the tent and, I imagine, pretty silly-seeming to those outside it. As for the latter, it's an occupational hazard of running experiments with children, experiments that have to make sense to them as games, to have them derided as silly. I first heard this, before I had ever ran an experiment, from the lips of an undergraduate biochemist in 1969, then it popped up frequently in the feedback sheets on my Glasgow lectures; and it has been a background rumble ever since. This is the defence: if you can't see any point in studying, say, the development of deductive reasoning in middle childhood, then hold your tongue, as it will all be silly *a priori* to you; if, however, you do see some point in studying it then you must agree that it is not worth doing unless you do it properly and nail it down. As you try to nail it down the studies will get progressively divorced from the everyday and more seemingly-solipsistic. Well that's the price of doing it properly. In any event, I could not see the silly side of the experiments I was doing around this time on non-verbal performance in length conservation (conservation failers can do it non-verbally, yet they then tell you how they did it!), and on transitive reasoning (showing that Peter Bryant seemed to be wrong in arguing that younger children failed because of poor short-term memory).

Meanwhile, inside the tent there was a kind of battle, not so much raging, as wittering. In those days most cognitive-developmental psychology was done within the context of Piagetian theory, so that even those who rejected it expended their energy in dismissing it rather than striking out into new territory. In the UK these dismissers clustered around the work of somebody who was not really a dismisser at all — Margaret Donaldson from Edinburgh. Margaret had a deep understanding of Piaget's theory. However, in her little book, *Children's Minds*, she made the point in a thorough but over-stated and over-charming way that sometimes children give the wrong answer not because they don't understand the principle involved but because, being children, the questions don't make "human sense" to them. There is some truth in this of course. However, the proof of the pudding lies in showing that they can pass the tests when they are framed by human sense; and here the results were puny, or impossible to replicate, or both.[53]

I knew which side of the debate I was on and it had to be the opposite one from those talking about "negotiating meanings" between child and experimenter. These people paid lip serve to the Donaldson position. Predictably enough to those who have shared this journey so far, I was dead-set against the sociologising of developmental experiments. That child is not negotiating a meaning: he is chewing on a Jammy Dodger whilst half-listening to you.

In any event, around this time I got to know some local developmental psychologists and I visited Geneva (though not to see Piaget). Both events only served to reinforce my "depressive position" in relation to cognitive developmental work. In the first place, Peter Lloyd from Manchester organised the North West Developmental Group, which brought together in a series of seminars developmentalists from Liverpool, Manchester, Lancaster, Keele, and Bolton. Socially they could be fun; intellectually they could be grim. Two of them stick in the mind. In one, we had a visiting speaker talking about children's failure to understand the locutionary force of words

---

[53] James McGarrigle and Margaret Donaldon argued that children change their answers in the number conservation experiment because the experimenter made the change – and so it seems important to acknowledge it in their answer. In support of this they found that if a "naughty teddy" made the change errors were fewer. However, Chris Moore and Doug Frye showed the effect was an artefact: the teddy event simply distracts them so they repeat "same": they *also* repeat "same" if teddy really adds more to one row. C. Moore and D. Frye (1986) The effect of experimenter's intention of children's understanding of conservation. *Cognition, 22*, 283-298.

like "all" (are all the cars in the garages? Not if there are empty garages. Do all the garages have cars in them? Not if there are un-garaged cars). While this does not set the pulse racing, in the discussion the worst — anyone up for some meaning negotiating? — were "full of passionate intensity." My temper was saved up to be lost at home, ranting to Chris as she sorted out our second child (Patrick, born in 1977). Inebriated by the exuberance of my own verbosity I even derided them as "jeans-wearing." She said: "What are those things on your legs?"

In another meeting we were debating what was the most common way for children to justify a non-conserving answer, till Andy Young (p.140 above) just said in exasperation: "Oh they say all kinds of things." Andy seemed the most able of the developmental group, and indeed he was too able to bother with the low-key mish-mash. Meetings always ended in the pub, and when Andy was leaving to drive back to Lancaster he said he was tired of all these ideological wranglings and was getting more interested in the brain these days. He already had a grant to look at the development of brain lateralisation, which eventually lead him away from developmental and towards neuropsychology. And for every Andy Young who got out of it there must been thousands of clever undergraduates who never got into it in the first place, given the state of cognitive developmental research in those days.

As for the road to Geneva, I had been awarded a substantial grant by the Social Science Research Council (now the Economic and Social Research Council because, for Thatcherites, there is no such thing as society, so there can be no such thing as social science. Yes, I know Thatcher would have been at one with me on Peregrine Trotter and his pals; but even Hitler believed that 2+2 = 4).[54] This grant was to look at whether, as Piaget claimed, social interaction between young children who were *equally* ignorant about some principle would bring about agreement on the correct answer. I was a sceptic. For the disagreement to cause a Piagetian "disequilibrium" and therefore re-thinking the children would have to see the two answers *as* conflicting,[55] which suggests some grasp of the principle itself. We did not find any evidence for "two wrongs making a right" in this way, but did find that less competent children would comply with the answer of more competent, even if the less competent were more dominant in personality, suggesting that they recognised the right answer when they saw it (I still show the wonderfully funny videotapes of this work to undergraduates in practical classes. At one point a 5-year-old non-conserving Liverpudlian, who is failing to reach agreement with his non-conserving pal turns round and says "It's hard weeerrk this intit!").

Unbeknownst to me at that time, this kind of work was also being done in Geneva by social psychologists who were reaching the opposite conclusion, which was that "socio-

---

[54] This was Enoch Powell to Ludovik Kennedy when the latter accused him of saying that Hitler would have agreed with him about something.

[55] To illustrate, in length non-conservation a child, having been shown two sticks of equal length with their tips aligned says that one of them is longer when it is moved up an inch or so. But what if you have two non-conserving children facing the display from opposite ends (one from the top, one from the bottom)? They should disagree about which is longer. Will this lead them to realise that they can't both be right, so they could both be wrong? Will it lead them to become conservers? Not according to my experiments. The Genevens strongly disagreed.

cognitive conflict" was one of the principal engines of cognitive growth. In any case, their research was bad: wrongheaded in conceptualisation, poorly done, and so never published in decent journals. Wrongheaded? For these people, "conflict" could include disagreement between two children, one of whom *knew more than the other*; so any improvement would be likely to be caused by the process that I had identified: one child learning from another. Notwithstanding all this, I was delighted to be asked to a three-day workshop on "socio-cognitive conflict" in Geneva — indeed, I went to the trouble to make copies of a lot of my video-tapes and send them over before the meeting.

Most of the Genevan work had been done by Willem Doise and Gabriel Mugny. Doise could not be there till the last day, so the organiser was Mugny. I sensed antagonism from the second I met him, and antagonism there was throughout — of a low-key, implicit, wheedling variety that culminated in his manoeuvring my non-invitation to the party he hosted at his house on the last night. At coffee he would lead people away from talking to me and invite them. During the meeting we rarely crossed swords directly except at one point when he reinforced his tired whinge that our experiments were "a social situation" by saying, "*I have seen your tapes!*" To which I replied: "I know you have. I sent them to you."

Much of the memory of the meeting is a cartoon-vision of lookilikies: a social headbanger from a Glasgow Poly, who was Balzac; a German, who was Nogbad the Bad; a huge Italian, who was Bluto; a postgraduate student from Southampton with a footballer's mullet; while Edith Piaf from Paris made interminable speeches and worried charmingly about the lack of a proper pudding at lunch. I recall that, and the torrential rain, as I wandered the streets by myself as the others partied at Mugny's house. I recall nothing of the debate, except the appearance of Willem Doise on the final day, whose response to my presentation was as intelligent as Mugny's was, er, not. Willem was quite a different kettle of fish from his co-worker, and we had an interesting lunch at which he told me much that I *do* actually remember about what it was like to work with Le Patron.

I want to make it clear that this Geneva story has not been inserted as just another of my *o-me-miserum* vignettes. The attitude of Mugny and his social-Geneva colleagues was exemplary king-of-the-ghosts, in just this sense. The claim that children develop cognitively through socio-cognitive conflict, even if this is conflict between two children one of whom knows more than the other, was not in any sense a scientific theory, purely in virtue of how it was treated by the Genevans who held it. It was the foundation of their work, something between a catechism and a meal-ticket. It wasn't a defeasible hypothesis; and there were no open minds. I had plenty of faults as an experimenter back then, but I had an open mind. In some ways, "two wrongs making a right" would have been the more *interesting* outcome, though not my prediction, and if my conjecture had proved wrong then one would have had to accommodate to it. The difference between me and them was that they were in the grip of a particular view of *what humans are like* — they are social constructors of knowledge; sorry they just *are* — and I was testing an idea that I hoped to lead to something interesting. It was experimental psychology. You may say that this kind of distinction is hardly unique to psychology, but I suspect it is. When minds study the mind it's hard to shake the ghost of what you as a possessor of a mind think mental life is all about.

Finally, note the difference between the attitudes of Doise and Mugny, one open and interested, one closed and distrustful. You see, it is not just a matter of holding the right or the wrong positions: it is how you hold them — your "propositional attitudes" to them in the jargon. In other words, it all depends on the person. Psychology is a highly personalised endeavour; so I make no apology for my highly personalised text.

Heeeeere's....Jerry (Fodor); and two Austrians too

So cognitive developmental psychology was, by the mid-1970s, in need of both a kick up the backside and something new to think about. It needed, in fact, to be kicked up the backside whilst thinking hard. The kick was delivered by Jerry Fodor, quite simply, and the something-new-to-think-about was provided by two Austrians — Josef Perner and Heinz Wimmer; well actually by a set of people – all European. The kick meant: "You are doing cognitive-developmental psychology in an Empiricist[56] stupor. Wake up and see what does not work and what just *has* to be the case."

---

[56] The philosophical view that all knowledge is derived from perceptual experience.

The new domain of thought was the domain of the mind — I mean children's conceptions of it. Piaget's work had focussed on the development of knowledge of what Vygotsky called "scientific" concepts (physical world, space, time, cause, logic, and so forth) and it had, more or less, ignored children's knowledge of the mind, except to insist that their knowledge of other minds would be stymied by their "egocentrism" far into middle childhood.

To me, and to many of my colleagues in the late 1970s, Jerry Fodor represented The Enemy: the kind of person who did not believe in real mental development in the way we did. In the words of Stirling's Robin Campbell, expressed to me: "Fodor is a pest, though an interesting pest." The "interesting" could not be denied. Even somebody who hates nativism will find Fodor a beguiling writer. British philosophy had some fine writers of English, such as Peter Strawson and Henry Price, and American philosophy had some tending-to-brash, no-nonsense stylists like John Searle; but Fodor was something else again. His arguments moved very quickly and impatiently with a kind of North American swing; he did not merely dispose of his opponents: he ridiculed them (with "Granny" representing the timid, unimaginative and feeble Empiricist establishment). Indeed, he was not just witty but funny.

The book I loved to hate but loved to read was his *The Language of Thought.* Its stance on knowledge acquisition was the Platonic one that knowledge acquisition is impossible without the right kind of representational format on which new information can find purchase (this was Chomsky's Poverty of the Stimulus Argument (p.128) applied to concepts). How do children learn geometry and the lexicon of their native language? Because they have within them the resources to represent the information that's presented to them. They can learn the meaning of the word "cat," because they can think cat-thoughts, just as they can learn what "yellow" means because they can see what yellow things have in common (of course it's not as simple as that, and David Hamlyn's work on Aristotle, touched on above, asked whether this kind of nativism was inevitable, and asked it with reference to the Aristotelian concept of *epagoge* — essentially the principle of induction. It's a long story).

Fodor did not say all this with reference to Plato. The reference was to digital computers, or rather to a computer-mind analogy, which became known as "the computational theory of the mind." We all know that computers have to be programmed if they are to do anything. In those days it would have been with BBC Basic or Lisp, and nowadays it would be perhaps with C++. Well this programming is never going to work unless the computer has a *machine code*, written in a digital code, on which the programming language can, in the above phrase, find purchase. Analogising boldly to humans, Fodor argued that we too have a machine code that he called *the Language of Thought (LOT)*— the symbolic format in which we think and that we need to acquire language.

Now there is a way of presenting this kind of position that is fairly anodyne. Lets say that indeed children will never be able to learn the word "chair" unless they can think, in his example, "portable," "seat," and "for one;" and lets say that a child will never be able to acquire the verb to eat unless she knows that eating is a kind of action. So on this position, children will need some innate *set* of core concepts (about agency, number, objects, etc.) that they can *combine* to produce in the service of learning language (this is, roughly, Steven Pinker's kind of nativism). Fodor, though, was having none of that kind of pussyfooting, because — this is another challenge to common sense — for him the meanings of words are not *decomposable* into semantic components, or "semantic features" as psycholinguists call them. There are no true definitions and, in the title of one of his papers, "to kill" does not mean "cause to die." The upshot of all this is that the innate symbolic representations children need to learn the words "chair" and "eat" are the un-decomposable core meanings CHAIR and EAT; and so these concepts are innate. If so, as Fodor literally says in the book, "*All Concepts Are Innate.*" What about DOOR KNOB? Innate. What about HORSE? Innate. Well surely not CARBURETTOR? Innate too.

I have to say that the way I am presenting Fodor makes him sound like the Indian paterfamilias on a BBC sketch show called *Goodness Gracious Me*. This man believed all famous men and women were Indian. What about Gladstone? Indian. What about Madonna? Indian. Aristotle? Indian too. And, yes indeed, the position does sound like a *reductio ad absurdum* of nativism. In fact, Fodor was careful about what he meant by "innate" and he defended his position in his usual spirited way in a much later book called *LOT2*. Nativist that I am, I never warmed to this book: the rapid-fire debates with Granny became irritating and I resigned myself to being granny-enough to settle for Pinker-style nativism. I also remained unconvinced when he marched towards the sound of Darwinian gunfire in his book with Massimo Piatelli-Parmarini called *What Darwin Got Wrong*. Darwin was, for Fodor, a kind of Skinnerian who thought that species produced morphological "operants" (behaviours) that the environment selected, like the experimenter giving a sniffing-round rat a pellet of food. In fact, I suspect I am not working hard enough over more recent Fodor.

Massimo Piattelli-Parmarini edited an important and, to us stick-in-the-muds, depressing book in the late 1980 called *Language and Learning: The Debate Between Jean Piaget and Noam Chomsky.* This was the record of a workshop held in the *Bois de Boulogne* in which these too debated — plus a number of others including Jerry Fodor. Chomsky and Fodor ran rings around Piaget. This was, in part, because he was old and ill — he was to die in September 1980 — and because his theory did not have the resources to survive attacks from the two most intelligent and committed nativists on the planet. For the theory had nothing at all of interest to say about how children learn the grammar of their native language and it implausibly required children to have adequate motor skill if they are to develop mentally. I recall Fodor pressing Piaget on the latter point, forcing him to whittle down what he meant by "action" to something gossamer-fine and useless. In fact Fodor was very respectful of Piaget; and not, I hope, just because they both voiced theories that were significant challenges "common sense."

Not all developmentalists were discomforted by Fodor; and certainly Peter Bryant had no need to be. You may recall my discussion of Peter Bryant's lectures on transposition in the late

1960s (p.50) and his point that children cannot learn to think relationally by learning comparative terms like "bigger," because how will they learn these words in the first place. Jerry Fodor spent some time in Oxford in the 1970s and this, though surely not *only* this, may have lead him to write in *The Language of Thought:*

> "I know of only one place in the psychological literature where this issue has been raised. Bryant (1974) remarks: 'the main trouble with the hypothesis that children begin to take in and use relations to help them solve problems because they learn the appropriate comparative term like 'larger' is that it leaves unanswered the awkward question of how they learned these words in the first place' (p. 27). The argument generalises, with a vengeance, to any proposal that the learning of a word is essential to mediate the learning of a concept that the word expresses."

I have read out this passage to undergraduates so often I can recite it like *Invictus.*

At the time Fodor's nativism did not trouble me because I thought it was self-evidently absurd and would just go away in time. What did trouble me was the computational theory of the mind and the functionalist (p.133 above) position on the mind-body relationship that went along with it. This too struck me as self-evidently absurd, and more insidious. Maybe the computational theory of the mind could explain the mechanistic aspects of cognition such as syntactic parsing and some kinds of reasoning, what about our knowledge of the physical world, emotion... what about our beloved subjectivity in relation to a refractory reality; and what about — God help us — *experience*! Does this reduce to symbolic states of a computer!

Huh? Not only did I wear granny glasses (still do): I was Fodor's "granny" in her very self.

In those years I was all over the place in the sense that everything I wrote, including my book *Explaining Mental Life: Some Philosophical Issues in Psychology* (1984), was fuelled by strong negative intuitions. In the case of the book, it was animus against Fodor's computational theory of the mind, against the whole idea that the mind is comparable to a digital computer. Negative passion is not necessarily a bad thing (the book I am writing even as we speak), because passion of some kind should drive one on. However, to get from A to B you need *arguments*, otherwise it is just "intuition pumping," in Daniel Dennett's phrase; it is just the kind of thing I criticised Ray Tallis for doing. As Adam Morton wrote in an otherwise kind and generous review of the book: "when we want an argument, we get a list of famous names." The fact is, I don't really think like a philosopher, though I do — quite a different thing —like to philosophise. Wittgenstein said that when two philosophers meet each should say to the other: "Slow down." However, give me a philosophical idea and I speed up like the *Andrex* puppy. Only great philosophers like Fodor — Ross Harrison rightly described him as one of the "great philosophers" when he introduced him at Cambridge in 2004 — can do philosophy at speed, or seem to. Now back to psychology and the "something new to think about."

There was something in the developmental air in the late '70s – early '80s, and that was an interest in child's understanding of mental processes. Paul Harris from Oxford (one of the people in my career against whom I have measured myself, before giving up) was working on children's understanding of emotion and writing papers with titles like "The child as psychologist," Liz Robinson's work on children's referential communication asked questions about intended meaning, while the people working hard to show that children were not as "egocentric" as Piaget said they were confronted the consequence that therefore younger children must be pretty *good* at working out what others were experiencing — sometimes.

My own contribution to this was a study on children's understanding of what philosophers call "referential opacity," meaning (among others things) that when we preface a sentence by "Fred thought that..." then the complement will not be true unless it is constrained by what Fred knows. For example: "Oedipus was passionately in love with his mother" is true, whereas "Oedipus thought that he was passionately in love with his mother" is false. This is so because thinking means representing in a certain light — in the light of one's knowledge. I did not run the study very well, in the sense that my questions were too complex grammatically and I did not even act out the little stories with props. For this reason I overestimated the age at which children could do it. It was, though, clearly the case that the whole idea of the truth of a "mental utterance" being relative to the speaker's state of knowledge was something that younger children struggle with. It was as if they lacked the "theory of mind" — a phrase we knew David Premack was using to refer his work on chimps' understanding of the mental.

While my referential opacity study was sort-of getting there as a test of what children knew about mental representation, it was too linguistic-scholastic. We needed something more direct and punchier; but *what*? This was, if not uppermost in my mind as I set off for my first trip to North America in 1981, at least some background music. I went to a conference in Toronto in August 1981, then took the Greyhound to Sacramento to see happily-married Jan Lowen of Birkbeck/Wyndham-Lewis/BM fame, then back West-to-East on a low trajectory taking in Nashville and ending in New York for a month — hosted by John Broughton at Columbia and Katherine Nelson at City University of New York on 42nd Street. The trip was wonderful. I think British people with anti-American feelings, who see only monied loudmouths in London, should be made to take a long Greyhound journey to get to know the American working (and drifting) classes — a kind of community payback. And they shouldn't worry if they hear themselves being referred to by one of the guys at the back of the bus as "that pansy-assed motherfucker."

The long conversation I had with Jerome Bruner at The New School for Social Research paralleled in pleasure the one with Tom Bower in 1972. Though I have been fairly quiet about Bruner, he was a big influence, right from the time Peter Bryant recommended to me his co-written book *Studies in Cognitive Growth*. His concerns were the same as Piaget's, except for the admixture of Vygotsky and Chomsky and for the interest in educational theory. He was a colourful, invigorating writer; though it has to be said that sometimes you wondered if there was much determinate meaning beneath all the invigoration.

Anyway, I took him some ideas I had for tests of children's understanding of belief itself, not the separate question of whether they know the linguistic constrains on belief reporting. I had an inkling they were hopeless ideas, and Jerry agreed with me in the nicest possible way. Nonetheless, we found so much common ground that I felt I was still walking on it when I got the Greyhound back up to Toronto some weeks later.

Bruner has recently resigned from the Watts Chair in Oxford, rather a glorious niche. His niche at the New School was a hundred steps down from the glorious: a pokey office outside of which the secretary denied all knowledge of any "Jeremy(sic) Bruner." What went wrong at Oxford? In his biography *In Search of Mind* he says it was an "unhappy" department, in evidence for which he says that each research group tended to stick to its own table at coffee time. Surely, though, part of the problem was that he wasn't an experimental psychologist in the Oxford sense. Jerry was a wide-ranging facilitator of ideas. To the Oxford diehards, though, these ideas were more cooked-up than facilitated; and they over-reached themselves. Facilitate he did though: Mike Scaife's study of joint attention in mother-baby dyads, and some interesting work on mother-child turn-taking as a social underpinning for language development.

In writing this now I think of the mean-spiritedness that may have been displayed to Bruner in Oxford. Did many of them want to make life comfortable for him? And in saying this I find, as I think back on what I have written about ghost psychology, some evidence of a similar meanness of spirit in myself. Maybe it is the voice of the experimental psychologist labouring in the coal-mines of equipment-grant-getting and referee placating that baulks at the facile *gloire* of big ideas. In any case, the big ideas of Bruner were not the big ideas described by Fabian Klein, nor the big ideas of Peregrine Trotter on discursive psychology. Yes, Bruner was very friendly to the kind of notions fielded by John Shotter and Rom Harré about the social underpinning of psychological categories (and Shotter attended the seminars that Bruner organised at Oxford on social development), but Bruner was a student of mainstream cognitive development first and foremost.

But — still wriggling — I have to say that subsequent Bruner does not set the blood racing. One of his themes has been the importance of narrative in cognitive development, something that's hardly a Fodorian or Piagetian challenge to common sense. The situation of Bruner post-Oxford became that of an elder statesman who writes and lectures on the way things seem to him, who delivers wisdom. Almost inevitably, this is done at low pressure. In clear contrast, Freud spoke of psychology as being his "horse," by which he meant something that carried him forward like an obsession; and all his writings bear this out. It seems to me that unless reflective writing on psychology has this character, no matter how eloquent, humane, and nuanced, then it will have a ghostly character. Indeed another horse, the "bloody horse" of Roy Campbell, springs to mind here, the horse missing in a certain kind of would-be-fine writing:

You praise the firm restraint with which they write
I'm with you there, of course:

They use the snaffle and the curb all right,
But where's the bloody horse?[57]

Ghost riders in the sky, in fact.

To rein things back at this point, the upshot of my failing to come up with a good test of children's understanding of mental representation was, of course, that somebody else came up with one. It did not spring fully armed from their heads exactly, but Heinz Wimmer and Josef Perner published an immaculately done and beautifully-argued paper on what has become known as "the false belief task." The idea is that if a child has a concept of belief then she will, as beliefs are only *in the running* for truth not true in themselves, have a concept of *false* belief, and to study this one can find out if she knows that if people have a false idea about where something is they will search for it in the wrong place. In their task, Maxi puts his chocolate in cupboard A and then goes out to play. When he is outside, his mum — there is a cover story — moves the chocolate from cupboard A to cupboard B. Maxi comes back in wanting his chocolate. First the child is asked some memory/comprehension questions: Where is the chocolate now? Where was it to begin with? Did Maxi see it move? Despite getting these questions right, 3 year olds will usually say that Maxi will look in cupboard B — where the chocolate really is, not where he should falsely belief it is. Four year olds do not make this error; so it seems they can operate with the concept of false belief, and thus of belief, and thus of mental representation *per se*.

---

[57] This is Roy Campbell's squib about certain South African writers.

It is no exaggeration to say that this work opened the floodgates. The field of autism was profoundly affected by it, and "theory of mind" replaced Piagetian concerns at the centre of cognitive-developmental research and teaching. Subsequently, Josef Perner has steadfastly maintained his 1983 position, while Heinz Wimmer moved on to work in other areas, such as children's reading. I might say that, in addition to Paul Harris (p.155 above), Josef is another developmentalist I used to measure myself against, before thinking better of it. We were born within a couple of weeks of each other and tend to be interested in the same kind of things. Where he has rock-like consistency I keep changing my mind and find myself holding conflicting positions in parallel. We were on a panel at a meeting in Florida once where he made an aside about "one of the many positions Jim currently holds." And it's not just that: his work has a rigour and empirical fecundity that most of us can only aspire to.

Before he did the false belief work with Heinz, Josef came to give a seminar on his ideas about the conservation task in Liverpool; and we put him up in Chester. This sticks in my mind as the occasion when our daughter Charlotte, who was about eight or nine at the time, decided to display some adult social skills, joining the conversation at the table with interjections of, "Really?" and, "Oh how odd!" listening with smiling vigilance. She would become his student at Sussex ten years later.

Dutch jobs, "Marty Wilde" jobs, and being below average

It almost goes without saying that I applied for other jobs while at Liverpool. The application process for one of them introduced me to the concept of a "Dutch job," paralleling Dutch courage in not being the real thing. The department of developmental psychology in Amsterdam wrote to me and asked if I could recommend somebody whom they might approach to apply for its Chair of Developmental Psychology. Unencumbered by modesty, I replied that I would like to recommend myself, particularly as the teaching could be done in English. I gave a good job-talk (no boozing the night before), was interviewed, and was offered the job. There was, though, one further step, which was that they had to write to universities in the UK and Holland in case anybody objected to their choice. To cut it short, people did indeed object, and so they sent me a further letter saying that there was "no chance" now that they could appoint me because respondents had said my CV was too thin and that I was not the person to conduct academic business in a foreign language. No doubt this was somebody who had attended one of my car-crash-talks and who thought that if he has this much trouble speaking English, then God help him in Dutch. A let-down then, and a disappointment for my family as well as for me. Patrick, who was a hamster enthusiast, had been looking forward to living in "Hamsterdam."

In the early 1980s the now-legendary Oxford philosopher
Gareth Evans[58] died. Evans had held the dream job for anybody
like me who fancied himself as living at the intersect of
psychology and philosophy — The Wilde Readership in Mental
Philosophy (or the Marty Wilde Readership as certain frivolous
people call it). I applied and was shortlisted. The Wilde
Professorship (as it is now) is a strange kind of job. The holder
is attached to the Department of Experimental Psychology and
yet is required to lecture on theoretical aspects of psychology
and debarred from — I forget the exact form of words —
"entering the laboratory." It is really a job for a philosopher
who engages with psychology — the last two have done that
brilliantly — rather than for somebody like me, a psychologist
who enjoys philosophy and likes to look for the empirical cash-
value in what philosophers say. The interview was
extraordinary. Here was Nick Mackintosh (p.35), co-opted
from Cambridge, Donald Broadbent (with whom I began this
narrative), Larry Weiskrantz (p.43), as well as some of the best
philosophical minds in Oxford — Peter Strawson , Michael
Dummett, Jennifer Hornsby and others lost in the mists of
memory. While I didn't disgrace myself at the interview, I had
made the mistake of sending them the Introduction to my
Explaining Mental Life, which had just come out, and in which
I had said some pretty silly things. One such silliness Peter
Strawson read out to me, which was something about the
functionalist theory of mind being consistent with dualism (p.

---

[58] Evans died tragically young. He was a neo-Kantian philosopher (a student of
Peter Strawson) whose great work (edited after Evans' death by John McDowell)
was on reference — *Varieties of Reference* (rather a Russellian view of it).

133 above). My attempt to defend myself, and in particular my saying that on functionalism mental states are "free-floating entities" gave Strawson the giggles. I made a decent fist of answering Nick's questions about the philosophy of animal learning, and I hear he and one or two other psychologists did indeed support me. It was clear from the philosophers' demeanour, however, that the only way they would agree to appoint me was if they were forced to appoint either me or, say, Alan "Fluff" Freeman. In any case, I had every intention of carrying on with my empirical work as both the dyadic interaction work and the mental language work were going well. And how could I do this without "entering the laboratory." Indeed, this would even have debarred Fodor, who did empirical work in psycholinguistics.

It took ages for them to turn me down, because the psychologists had refused to agree to the appointment of Christopher Peacocke, whose philosophical turbo-charge left them uncomprehending. A compromise had to be reached and this was Colin McGinn, who had at least done a degree in psychology. I later met him at a workshop on theory of mind that Paul Harris had organised at St. John's. Well… I can almost go on automatic pilot to type that the night before my talk scheduled for 9.00 on Sunday morning there had been a party at Paul's, at which much wine had been drunk by me. In reaction to my struggled articulations that Sunday morning McGinn laughed, and not small Strawsonian giggles. He laughed as if somebody had punched him in the stomach while he was trying to force a chip down his nose. In later years I have enjoyed McGinn's often beautifully articulated and witty criticisms of other philosophers, criticisms that can also be terminally contemptuous. Since my experience of him that Sunday morning I've regarded the latter as springing not only from the intellectual aggression to which we're all prone, but also from something darker.

The week of this workshop, one of a number that lead to Paul's edited book with Janet Astington and David Olson, *Developing Theories of Mind,* had been a bad one for me and a bad one for the Liverpool Psychology department. I forget what it was called in those days, and even now it keeps changing its name. Just to say that this was the year (1985?) of the first "Research Assessment Exercise" in which all university departments in the UK were ranked in terms of their research quality. We were ranked Below Average, along with – I think – Swansea and one or two others. These research assessment exercises have long fallen into contempt among independently-minded academics, despite the fact that so much hangs on them. Their first appearance in the mid-'80s came as a wake-up water-canon to certain departments. Independent mindedness was the last thing I felt capable of when I heard the news. My first thought was: "How did they know?"

Not: how did they know about the department? But, how did they know about *me?* How did they know that while I was doing well getting research money from the SSRC/ESRC, while I had published in good journals and had written some thoughtful books and theoretical papers that really I deserved to be where I was, among people who only came in during the vacation to water their plants? How did they know that my response to the theory-of-mind revolution was that of a small-p piagetian stick-in-the-mud (witness my chapter in the Astington et al book mentioned above)? How did they know that I was trying to carve a little research niche for myself out of thin air, a doomed attempt to apply Johnson-Laird's mental model's theory [59] to sentence verification tasks in young children? How did they know I actually thought this work had a kind of rigour that theory-of-mind-work lacked? How did they know I was running these reaction-time experiments with kids using the blinking green idiocy of an *Amstrad* computer? How did they know that some vacation days I simply could not face the journey into Liverpool and stayed at home typing a lifeless novel?

A staff meeting was called to discuss the bombshell-which-should-not-have-been, at which those who spoke did so with one voice: 'They've got it wrong!' When the Faculty (of Social Studies) asked for our response to this grading our response was itself below average. One of the points we made was that people just have no idea how *long* psychological research takes, including in the list of research tasks "participants have to be thanked." We also made the point that, indeed, our research income was low — I was the only person during my time there who had gained external funding — but just look how much research we've managed to do without it! The ethos was comical. Here is some ethos in "vivid detail" (as social psychologists call it). In the meeting somebody said this about applying for research grants: "You can spend all your time on

---

[59] The idea that the basic representational format for deductive and other reasoning is a concrete "mental tableau" and that the better the reasoner you are the more of these possible tableaux you iterate.

the application and then not get it." In other words, trying is a waste of time because you may fail.

I had been trying to leave Liverpool for the past ten years — only some of my attempts have been mentioned — and at last I succeeded. After a failed attempt to get a job in the Cambridge Department posing as a psycholinguist, I was offered a Lectureship in developmental psychology in 1987.

Christine was not keen on moving. There were all kinds of official and unofficial reasons for this, but the main one was that our marriage was fading away.

Cambridge: Gateway to Kings Cross

Ontological trees in the bat-cave

Strolling through cloistered quads with like-minded people, then to enjoy sumptuous food and fine wines in chiaroscuro? No. Waking in digs, too far out of town, my room next to the kitchen so that it stank of bacon fat and *HP Sauce*; then into the department to spend the day failing to find my feet, lunching alone in the *Copper Kettle* across from Kings, like a tourist. Perhaps there is a literary form even lower than the misery memoir, which is the misery memoir of a cosseted academic mixing personal with intellectual misery; maybe he even "brags about his misery" when it was simple ambition that made him live hundreds of miles away from his family.

Actually, things were not so bad. It was a happy department, and it was great to be back within Nick Mackintosh's ambit. My colleagues were welcoming, especially Paul Whittle, Stephen Monsell, Tony Dickinson, Peter Cooper, Joan Stevenson-Hinde from the Sub-Department of Animal Behaviour, as well as more junior people like Cecilia Heyes, and Cathy Urwin (the latter from the Childcare and Development Group over in the Social Sciences Faculty). I was not, though, in a good situation. How could I be, with Charlotte (13) and Patrick (10) so far away? The sensible strategy would have been to throw myself into my research. But that would have been like taking a high dive into the shallow end.

Looking back, if I had any overarching research strategy at all it was to do anything that happened to take my fancy as long it had nothing to do with theory of mind. I felt that I had missed the wave here, and was left paddling out to sea as the central theorists — Josef Perner, Alan Leslie, and Paul Harris — surfed in. OK, I would make my own wave then. Research into children's understanding of tautology and contradiction (my soporific job talk), studying reaction-times in sentence-verification tasks within a mental models framework (already mentioned), and — see below —piggy-backing on Frank Keil's interesting work on children's ontological categories? These could only make ripples.

Turning to the final ripple, just before I left Liverpool the ESRC had given me a two-year grant to look at children's understanding of ontological constraints on predication, on their ability (remarkably good) to judge that "the cow lasts for two hours" is "silly," but "the cow is purple" is "OK." From quite a young age they know that certain predications are fitted to certain kinds of entity and not to others. The project also included plans for further work on children's understanding of disjunction (begun in the sentence-verification experiments), in particular on their grasp of exclusive disjunction (A or B, not both) compared to inclusive disjunction (A or B or both). Doesn't exactly set the blood racing does it? I think my obsession with "or" was fuelled by a thought that it was a "pure" form of abstract concept, in the sense of not being visualisable in a single image (unlike "and").

As just touched on, it was the American Frank Keil who had made the original move in the ontology work. He introduced an "ontological tree" with "all things" at the top bifurcating down via "things with spatial location" versus "abstract objects" to "animals" bifurcating down to "sentient beings" versus "non-sentient beings." This in turn gives rise to a "predication tree," given that predicates appropriate to entities higher on the tree such as "lasts for two hours" (events) cannot be applied to entities lower on the tree (animals) — hence the constraint that "the cow lasts for two hours" violates. Keil's message was one of competence: young children's trees are just "collapsed" versions of the adult tree; and indeed this fits in with more recent work with pre-schoolers by Nancy Soya[60] showing that their grasp of ontological types is remarkably good. I was, however, not convinced by the Keil work and planned to do semantic-generalisation experiments where children had to select pictures of the same kind of entity, because I thought this method was more appropriate and rigorous than silly/OK judgements. While this was a sensible enough move the whole thing turned out to be a resounding flop. Before me is a reprint of the only paper I published on the work entitled "Up and down the ontological tree: categories and semantic generalisation" a paper I simply cannot bear to read because it

---

[60] See Nancy Soya's work on understanding ontological categories in very young children: Soja, N. N. , Carey, S. & Spelke, E. (1991) Ontological categories guide young children's inductions of word meanings. *Cognition, 38*, 179-211.

evokes such a hateful period — personally and intellectually hateful. The personal and the intellectual were two categories I could not separate on my tree, at least at that time. Perhaps the same goes for now.

One of the most important decisions a psychology researcher makes is made in appointing a research assistant or post-doc to a grant. Appoint the wrong person and your life can become a living hell, especially if your group is a small one. This is what I did in 1987 (and did it again in 2010). Rita Hawksmoor* was not really a psychologist at all. If she has to be categorised she would be just below ghost-psychologist on the relevant tree — *vampire*-psychologist. I invited a vampire-psychologist into the bastion of flesh-and-blood psychology because otherwise, as is the ontological constraint on vampires, she would have remained howling in the cold. In appearance she was bat-like, always black-clad; and she sucked all life out of the work, or at least out of my enthusiasm for it (did she spend her nights looking for two-hour-lasting cows on which to piggy-back for blood?).

So why was she ever appointed? Because in the interview she seemed to be feisty and fun, and somebody I could get along with. Perhaps she would be a welcome change too from what I thought of as the austerity of the department. On paper she was good: First Class degree from a good psychology department and coming with a strong recommendation from somebody I respected highly. She was just finishing a Ph.D. in Oxford in the Linguistics Department on some aspect of sociolinguistics; but she swore undying love for ontological categories. I recall the interview as little more than sharing gossip about Oxford and recall that I did most of the talking. In fact, I never really interviewed her at all.

Difficult as it is, I will park the personal "issues" with Rita and focus on the intellectual, opening a door on a particular kind of ghost psychology. One of Rita's Ph.D. supervisors had been Roy Harris, then Professor of General Linguistics at Oxford — which should have sounded a warning bell. I only knew Harris through reading his head-bangingly anti-Chomsky book reviews in literary journals like the *TLS*. One in particular sticks in my mind in which he compared Chomsky to an octopus squirting a black ink of technical obfuscation in the eyes of his critics as it scuttled away across the ocean floor. Everything he said about Chomsky was proof he didn't actually understand what Chomsky was doing — didn't see the point of it. Much of his writing was about Ferdinand de Saussure, who has always seemed to me an overrated figure in the history of linguistics (the punning title of one of Ray Tallis's books — *Not Saussure*). And if he had a philosophy behind his linguistic ideas it was that of the behaviourist, aligning himself with what the so-called logical behaviourism of Ryle. Of course, the behaviourist struggles with the whole idea of word meaning as a mental representation and so Harris — I cannot find where he says it, but others say he says it, and so did Rita — claimed that actually words don't have meaning. *Yeah.*

What follows now is the linguistic equivalent of Jonathan Harker creeping around a dank basement in Dracula's castle ... Rita told me, once she was safely in post, that actually the "empirical" part of her Ph.D. was not yet done and would I mind if she did it when there was a lull in her work for me? Of course I minded ... I said I would stay off the personal stuff. The plan was to show participants clips from a fly-on-the-wall documentary from the 1970s called *The Family* so they could assess how the members of this rough-and-ready family from Reading *negotiated the meanings of words*. Harker turns to the camera and screams.

Before we stopped talking to each other after a dreadful row, Rita had tried to engage me in the meaningless-words question. Rita was in fact of middle-class origin, while her mode of speech was faux-working-class inarticulate. Was she too busy negotiating meanings inside her head to speak in her normal way? No, I think she believed that interjecting lots of "sorta-likes" made her sentences sound like the product of unmediated, primitive intuition, of raw-honest thought. "Words sorta-like don't actually have a meaning, if you, like, think about it." I can see her standing beside my filing-cabinet saying this as the department rumbled on in its blessed sanity.

There are positive things to be said about Rita and her subsequent career (in something well-earthed and useful), but this is not her role in my narrative. Where people like Peregrine Trotter at least believe what they say and have intellectual energy, the Rita Hawksmoors who burrow through the rotten timber of academia have the deadly blend of dishonesty and the knack of exploiting situations and people. In my vulnerable state I had been rich for exploitation.

The Windows Task and Autism

Things could only get better; and they did. The weekends I didn't spend in Chester I spent in London. On my 40th birthday I went down to the Lyric Hammersmith to see Simon Callow star in a wonderful production of *Faust* — the whole darn thing, taking up much of the day. I had also, by now, joined the graduate College Clare Hall as a Fellow and Tutor. Clare Hall is a small, informal, likeable place. I enjoyed my time there, no less than when I revived my Am-Dram career playing Harold Gorringe in Peter Schaffer's *Black Comedy*. Gorringe is an overtly gay, Northern antique dealer. Some Clare-Hallites complained I did not camp it up sufficiently. Well, given that my first relationship after Christine had just bitten the dust I didn't want to give certain female persons the, uh, wrong idea. At one point Harold says to the young husband spitefully: "You deseeeerve each oooother, you and that little *nit!*" This has remained with me. Few people I know well have never heard me deliver it with real camp venom — a fine defuser of tension.

Life was unpredictable in a way it could never have been back in the North West. It was certainly unpredictable too that a distinctive position attached itself to me within the theory of mind area. Two things spurred this on. One was being asked by Katherine Nelson to write a review of the three main theory-of-mind collections for the journal *Cognitive Development*. My title was "The Theory Theory: So good they named it twice?" (p. 123 for the term "theory theory"). I can't say I like this long review when I look at it now — having, as it does, an unearned *de haut en bas* quality (I later felt I had to apologise to Henry Wellman). It also had a stuffy tone, well captured by something one of my graduate students, Claire Hughes, said to me about it: it was like the conversation of Victorian gentlemen looking on as the mothers and children played further down the beach. At least it served the purpose of making me think hard.

The second spur towards theory-of-mind work was purely empirical. A final-year project I supervised in 1988-9 was one inspired by a famous but problematic study by David Premack[61] on the chimpanzee theory of mind. Premark rightly argued that having a concept of false belief, which is the core of theory of mind, is required for lying, given that lying is implanting a false belief in another person's mind. Premack showed that chimps can learn (over a period of nine months) to deceive an antagonistic trainer in order to obtain food. The clear problem is that all they may have been doing in fact was learning to do something to get a reward, with no "mentalising" (in the jargon) strategies needed at all. My idea was to do a study similar to Premack's with preschool children who are on the cusp of passing Wimmer and Perner's canonical test of false belief. Will the 4 year olds pass and the 3 year olds fail? My crucial modification was that my subjects were never rewarded for the deceptive act of pointing to the empty box.

Children played a game for sweets against an opponent, with one undergraduate being the tester and the other the opponent. Both players closed their eyes as the tester hid a

---

[61] Woodruff, G. and Premack, D. (1979) Intentional communication in the chimpanzee: The development of deception. *Cognition, 7,* 333-363. The phrase "theory of mind" was not coined in this paper but in another one by these authors in *Brain and Behavioural Sciences*.

Smartie in one of two closed boxes between them. The child then has to point to one of the boxes to tell the opponent which one to open. If the child happened to point to the one with the *Smartie* in it, causing the opponent to open the box, then the chocolate went to the opponent. But if, by good chance, the child had pointed to the one that was empty, so the opponent opened it, the child won the chocolate. The 3- and 4-year olds played this for a few trials and were pretty happy to win about half of the chocolates. Note that what the child has learned here is: "It's in my interest to lure the opponent to the empty box, but I don't happen to know which the empty one is, before I point." Given this, the child is *never rewarded* for intentionally pointing to the empty box, because the child is not able to point to it with any certainty.

What happens next is that the child is told that this time it will be easier to win as the experimenter swaps the boxes for ones containing windows facing towards the child and away from the opponent. The interest, at least initially, was in what children would do on the first trial. Would they point to the empty box now they know which one was indeed empty? The initial results showed that, indeed, the 3-years-olds were *not* doing this. They pointed to the box that they could now see had a *Smartie* in it; whereas the 4-years-olds tended to do the rational thing and point to the box they now know to be empty. However, after these data started to come in I told the students to run some more children to see if the ones who were pointing to the "baited" (to use the language of animal learning) box could *learn* to point to the empty one, just like Premack's chimps did. So they were given 20 trials after the boxes were swapped for windowed ones. What was clear, as well as clearly remarkable, was that generally the younger ones who had pointed to the *Smartie*-box on the first trial continued to do this for all 20 trials. They clearly had not gone off chocolate and they could plainly see that in pointing directly to what they wanted they lost it and stopped winning *Smarties*. I decided to check what was going on so I went into the nursery myself and found exactly the same thing.

The initial finding, before the further 20 trials were added in, looked like something easily explicable in terms of a theory-of-mind challenge: the children were failing to point to the empty box because they did not know what it meant to implant a false belief ("It's in there!") into the mind of somebody. But when we add in the (in the jargon) "perseveration" — I mean the pointing to the baited box for 20 trials as if they could not help it — it looks far more like the kind a thing that patients with lesions of the pre-frontal cortex do: the blind repetition of an action not in their interest. In fact, it looked like a deficit in so-called *executive functioning*, meaning the *control* of action and thought, in stark contrast to the kind of *conceptual* impairment that the false belief task seemed to be unearthing.

After Finals we thought is would be a good idea if we all — me too — tested some children with autism on this task, given the research by people at the MRC Cognitive Development Unit — Alan Leslie, Simon Baron-Cohen, and Uta Frith[62] — showing that children with autism need a mental age far higher than 4 to pass the false belief task, if they passed it at all. In

---

[62] Baron-Cohen, S., Leslie. A. and Frith, U. (1985) Does the autistic child have a theory of mind? *Cognition, 21*, 37-46.

fact, the CDU people had designed the study to test the idea that theory of mind is the core impairment in autism – a brilliantly provocative and inspirational notion.   By some process I have forgotten, a jolly fellow called Tom Tidswell, a medic who had just finished his psychology degree, lent his help and his car. Tom used to pick me up in this car in the early morning and we would travel south, past what he called "the bread-basket of England," to a small town in which there was a school for children with autism (as we drove through the quiet, early-morning Cambridge streets I used to imagine, in order to maintain a proper sense of absurdity, a Hollywood feature being made of all this with Jack Nicholson playing me and Tom being played by Tom Hanks. The title of the film would be borrowed from Jerry Bruner's autobiography *In Search of Mind.* Tom's car would be an E-Type Jag, and I would climb aboard saying: "Tom. Let's go… *in search of mind*").

   In testing the children in the school I felt something similar to what I had felt with the schizophrenics in Tooting Beck. Similar, but different. Similar, because I felt I didn't belong in a clinical environment. Different because, in meeting a schizophrenic one felt "here is a person gone wrong," whereas in meeting a person with autism one felt "this is a completely different kind of person." It was not, by the way, that I shun challenging populations on principle. When I was a Ph.D. student in London I taught skinheads in a school in Kings Cross. This was challenging enough, and I made a pretty poor fist of it. With children with autism it was not just that I tested them poorly — one of the graduates said I was too gentle with them — it was that I found their psychological distance from me disturbing.

To cut it short, the children with autism behaved like our 3 years olds, despite having verbal mental ages much higher than 3; whereas a control group of children with Down's Syndrome behaved like our 4 year olds if they had mental ages of at least 4. We published the study, calling our task The Windows Task.[63]

You did not have to be a genius to develop a distinctive position on theory of mind research out of these data, albeit a rather reductive, if not debunking, approach. It was not an exciting position as it was essentially about the *brakes that have to be released* for mental development to happen. It became known as the *executive* position. To explain: one of the central requirements of an efficient executive system is to inhibit *wrong and strong* responses: to stop doing the very thing that habit and some salient stimulus in the world tells you to do. This is called inhibiting the "prepotent response." With regard to the Windows task the prepotent response is to point to what you want — the chocolate — not to the location that does *not* show what you want. Given this, it is possible that 3-year-old children and people with autism may actually understand what it means to lie, but when push comes to shove, just can't help but do the wrong thing. They lack self-control, not an insight into "mentalising." And given this, the same argument can be applied when explaining why 3 year olds and children

---

[63] Russell, J., Mauthner, N., Sharpe, S. & Tidswell, T. (1991) The 'windows task' as a measure of strategic deception in preschoolers and autistic subjects. *British Journal of Developmental Psychology, 9*, 331-349.

with autism fail the false belief task. Recall that in Wimmer and Perner's false belief task Maxi returns to the kitchen falsely believing that his chocolate is in cupboard A when in fact his mum has moved it over to cupboard B. Where will he look? Well, the child knows where it is (at B) so that's where his attention might be focussing, and it is also where Maxi ought to look; so referring to that place can be considered the prepotent response. In other words, children of 3 years of age and perhaps even people with autism may indeed understand how false beliefs function within the mental economy, while failing to control themselves sufficiently well to inhibit reference to the focal object in the task — the chocolate.

So what develops? On one version of the executive approach nothing much develops at all between 3 and 4 years beyond the ability to control yourself. So, is mental development really a matter not of developing conceptual insights but of children developing the ability to act on knowledge they already have? That's what I meant earlier when I said that on this view development is a matter of which brakes have to be released — executive ones. Taking a view like this rather went against the grain for me, as instinctively I believe in the reality of conceptual change and bridle at debunking accounts of why children fail the major tests.

I used to try to joke about my new debunking self. "As Jackie Charlton [football manager at that time, brother of Bobby] once said, 'I'm a nega'ive thinker me!' " — that kind of thing. I used to write anonymous conference sketches for the BPS Developmental Section Newsletter at that period, which were gonzo-of-imagination though not of fact. In one report of a Seattle conference I said within a fantasy: "Never Mind the Bollocks, It's the Executive Functions;" and, indeed, half of me did think something like that — while the other half was lampooning myself.

In fact, I think now that the executive position, as I used to express it, had a kind of energising naïveté that puts me in mind of what John Broughton (my host at Columbia on my first American adventure) said to me once. He said that theories in cognitive science/experimental psychology have "a kind of built-in obsolescence." He was making the point in favour of what he would call a "critical psychology" and thus against cognitive science/experimental psychology; while for me it is in a point *in favour* of the kind of psychology I try to do. In a young science you climb using the ladder at hand, throw it away, and look for the next ladder. That's how it is in young sciences (more about the executive theory and the whole idea that *Im Amfang war die Tat*,[64] later). One of the things that is so awful about ghost psychologies, in contrast to this, is their ability to last forever. They are undead.

In relation to what did the executive theory stand? In a nutshell, there were four main approaches to theory-of-mind development. Josef Perner's view that what was acquired was something broader — a theory of representation itself — in photos, films, sentences, not only of mental representation. He called this "meta-representation:" the child's ability to represent mentally the representing relationship between a belief (or photograph etc.) and a situation. Alan Leslie's view

---

[64] "In the beginning was the deed" – Goethe's *Faust*.

was the explicitly nativist one that early intimations of theory-of-mind can be seen when children engage in pretend/symbolic play. Thus, if a child pretends, or appreciates another's pretending, that a banana is a telephone (his example) then there is evinced some grasp of how a representation ("telephone") can be decoupled (his term) from reality, rather as mental representations are decoupled from reality, with the decoupled representation being that which is acted on. Alan's paper in *Psychological Review*[65] setting out this view is surely one of the great papers in developmental psychology. Paul Harris's view was that no theory-like insights are involved at all. Instead, children, in working out what another person thinks (or what they used to think themselves), use imaginative projection to simulate the other's mind, setting aside the default of what they currently think themselves. He describes this as "the work of the imagination" (a phrase I have only encountered in William Carlos Williams; though Paul did not take it from him). This distinction between "the theory theory" and what became known as "simulation theory" set the philosophers to work; and indeed it runs deep, being one aspect of the division in the social sciences and history between *Naturwissenschaft* and *Verstehen*.[66]

The approach — the fourth — of Alison Gopnik (the only American among the-usual-suspects) is by far the most

---

[65] Leslie, A. M. (1987) Pretence and representation: the origins of theory of mind *Psychological Review, 94,* 412-426.

[66] The philosopher Jayne Heal has written insightfully about this distinction as it applies to the mental domain: "Understanding other minds from the inside" in her collection *Mind, Reason, and Imagination*, Cambridge University Press.

provocative. It is "theory theory" to the max. Not only do children acquire a theory of mind at the age of 4: it is a theory that they have devised by themselves, by virtue of their natural capacity for asking questions about why people do what they do. They hit upon the theory theory because it is the most plausible way of explaining the data. This seems to entail that they have within them a brilliant homuncular scientist who sifts the data and constructs theories to fit it. I used to think that this was absurd until I reminded myself that I was happy with Chomsky's idea (not his way of putting it!) of a brilliant *linguist* inside the child so why not extend the courtesy to Gopnik's view? She did not regard children's "starting state" as a blank slate and said that they begin life with a crude, not-good-enough theory which they abandon, rather like the ladders I talked about above.

I think most readers would regard the executive approach to development as pretty dull stuff compared to these four. Most readers would be right. I felt somehow lumpen making my points, even inside my own head. Though, as we shall see, with the admixture of Kant and a homeopathic dose of Piaget something interesting could be made of it. But first ...

Graduate students, and some pontificating about ghosts and literature in relation to science

I acquired a new graduate student for each of the first three years I was in Cambridge. Numbers one and three are now man and wife, while number two is married to one of her fellow Part II psychology undergraduates from her year. We don't just keep it in the family: we make it families out of "it." Names and pack-drill: Elisabeth Meins, Claire Hughes, Charles (Chas) Fernyhough. They are all quite well known now — all professors — with Chas's profile extending well beyond empirical psychology, given his novel-writing and engagement with the general public on the matters neuroscientific; and indeed his neuroscientific novel and general-reader-friendly books about mental development and memory. Chas is principal investigator on a big— £2,75 million — collaborative project funded by the Wellcome Trust on hearing voices. Next week (writing this in April, 2016) I am going to the launch of Chas's latest book *The Voices Within* at the Wellcome Collection. That the book is dedicated to me gives me enormous satisfaction.

Chas Fernyhough was the only one of my graduate students who reminded me of myself at that age. He was bookish, a lover of big theories that went against the grain, seemed to be searching for a central view of human mentality; and he was a great reader of novels — destined to become a writer of them, as I said (he was also loyal to me in the certain small ways that gladden a supervisor's heart). He certainly did not, as I did, come to psychology via literature, because he was studying

Natural Sciences and must surely have known from the start that psychology is a scientific discipline. His interest in literature did not run in parallel with that in psychology: one informed the other; or so it seemed, and seems to me now. Also, his guiding star was Vygotsky, as was mine in the late '60s. This remains true of him; and therein lies one of the differences between us. I chop and change, whereas he has remained true to his original position; indeed, you can say, he *has* a position. There is though a second difference, which is that Chas makes literature out of his intellectual passions, and I strive to keep the psychological sealed off from literature — from my small attempts at it.

I certainly don't want to ascribe positions to Chas he no longer holds, so I shall tread carefully now in making two points that spring from these memories: one about having what might be called "an over-arching view of mentality" and the other about mixing psychology and literature. There are dangers in both, I believe.

The "overarching view of mentality" first. The point about being any kind of " ...ian" or "...ist" is that you may be one for non-empirical but not philosophical reasons (I am not saying that this applies to Chas). In my career as an anti-nativist, a (small p) piagetian, a Vygotskyan, a Laingian, a kind of connectionist-empiricist, and one or two other things which have emerged or are to emerge from this narrative I was not one because of exposure to data or from hearing philosophical arguments. This is because they were not based on data, but were *applicable* to some kinds of data. They were positions that I happened to like. The fact that they are *not* applicable to other kinds of data can never trouble the sleep of the "...ian" or the "...ist." The beauty of experimental psychology, by contrast, is that it has no time for such attitudes; and this can be brought home to you sharply when you try to publish in decent psychology journals.

You may think this is dull and restrictive, a block on the imagination. In fact it sets the imagination free, free to consider, for example, that maybe children's private speech (a Vygotksyan idea) actually has *no* causal role to play in development at all, or that it may turn out that purely sub-symbolic computational models *can* indeed mimic the acquisition of syntax with no innate representations of what is to be learned — the examples almost generate themselves. Somebody who does psychology in the way I've come to think it should be done will have no dogmatic slumbers[67] from which he has to be awakened. Actually, it is not so much a question of being asleep: the "...ian" and the "...ist" is often the one in danger of living in a kind of stupor.

That said, I would regard myself as a nativist, as well as a kind of Chomskyan and Fodorian. How, then, was this feat achieved? Because these positions were arrived at via philosophy, which in turn informed my reading (and my believing) of the evidence. While, as we have seen, I cannot go the whole Fodorian hog in my nativism there is something right — I mean *a priori* right, not right after a look at the evidence — about the idea that some kinds of knowledge simply cannot be acquired from scratch. Could a child acquire a conception

---

[67] Kant said that reading Hume on causality awoke him from his dogmatic slumbers.

of a mind-independent external world, or conception of the mind itself, without some innate set of representations? In saying "No" I would cite philosophers not developmental studies. The difficulty arises when the "...ism" is not based on reading or thought but on raw intuition. As that fine student of language acquisition Leila Gleitman once said, "The trouble is, empiricism is innate."

Now to the question of mixing psychology and literature. What I certainly don't wish to say is that mixing them has to be a doomed project. It's merely a dismissive spasm to say that this mixing must fall short of doing what (say) novels and scientific psychology are designed to do: to create characters that are ends-in-themselves (rather than theory-bound ciphers); and to dig out some impersonal truths about mentality. In doing one you prevent the doing of the other, the sceptic moans. That certainly *is* a danger; but a writer of real talent can surely side-step it. Indeed, I would say that in Chas Fernyhough's novel *A Box of Birds* the danger is brilliantly overcome — both an exciting novel and food for thought. The novel succeeds in fictionalising the tension between what neuroscience tells us about ourselves ("just a bundle of neurones") and our sense of self-hood and autonomy.

But Chas and I differ here; and there is no way round it. I would never attempt the blending of psychology and literature. In psychological writing I like plainness. Am I the only one whose teeth are set on edge by the presence, in psychology books not books for the general reader, of sensitive, "fine" writing, larded with lessons from the classics? If you have something to say about psychology, then lets hear it plain.

"Well your own teeth must be on edge whenever you look over your own text!" No, this misses the target because this book is about how I came to a view about the nature of psychology: it presents no psychological theory. So let's move on shall we? "To where?" I think to a bit of social scene-setting, before we get back to the scientific story.

Just before we do though, I need to insert a further bit of self-defence. Towards the very end of this narrative I will pull back the velvet curtain and reveal some king-of-the-ghosts psychology in all its horror. And in doing so I will quote extensively from a chap-book-length poem I published in 2012 — an absurdist diatribe against a kind of "qualitative psychology." "So, if you have teeth prepare to have them have them set on edge *later*." Not really. Poetry (rather loosely applied term in this case) can be about anything (or nothing). If I were a plumber ("...*but then again no*") and wrote a poem against bad plumbing it would not be a hybrid of poetry and plumbing.

In my case, the divorce of literature from psychology had begun long ago, after going along to a reading by the poet Lee Harwood at University College Oxford one Saturday night in 1968. Psychological realism would kill this kind of poetry stone dead, depending as it does on the collaging of reality rather than thinking about it, a collaging that omits the poet as a judging, emoting, abstracting mind. This reading lead me on to a number of other poets and especially to the work of John Ashbery who said in one poem[68] "... *What is writing?/Well, in*

---

[68] John Ashbery 'Ode to Bill'in *Self Portrait in a Convex Mirror,* (Manchester: Carcanet, 1976), p. 50.

my case, it's getting down on paper/Not thoughts, exactly, but ideas, maybe:/Ideas about thoughts. Thought is too grand a word./Ideas is better, though not precisely what I mean./Some day I'll explain. Not today though." I am simply addicted to Ashbery's work in the way that other people of my generation are addicted to Bob Dylan's (In fact, I'm addicted to Dylan too).

Snobbery and the ghost

When I was an undergraduate at Oxford I encountered a fair amount of snobbery, not only aimed at working-class rough-necks like myself, but at scientists. Scientists were supposed to be from the North and to slave away in the labs of North Oxford all afternoon while the stylists, who languished in the Arts and Humanities, could go on the river or entertain ladies to tea. At least as a Bristolian from a comprehensive school I escaped categorisation as a Northern grammar school boy. I am reminded of the Larkin-Amis (when undergraduates at St John's) fantasy, of The Northern Scholar: "A thoorally grand tutorial that. Value for t'money."

Cambridge is a quite different kind of place from Oxford — see Kingsley Amis and Kenneth Tynan *passim* in their downgrading of the former — and, of course, one experience was in the '60s and the other in the '90s. I did encounter snobbery at Cambridge, though of a quite different kind: snobbery about colleges and how some fall short of the *gloire* of old stone and fine tradition (that both my examples involve the Irish has zero significance). In fact I have to own that the examples have *almost* no *prima facie* significance beyond their role of backdrop.

Both examples concern Clare Hall (p.174 above). Nobody could mistake Clare Hall for King's or Trinity. It is a small, red-brick, low-rise, rather modernist set of buildings giving an impression of cosiness when you enter it — standard lamps and swish curtains, soft furnishings, not oak and leather. It is a graduate college. In my first week as a Fellow the leader (President? Fuhrer?) of the student body, a young man from the Irish republic, like Bono but without the modesty, a man who one of his referees predicted would "jack-boot his way to the top," had written a document called "Clare *What*?" Somebody thought this grubby slice of spleen merited an extraordinary meeting between the tutors (including me) and the student body. The Irishman's job was easy, for all he had to do was to tap into a vein of anger among the overwhelmingly-overseas student body at the fact that they were students in a college that some minicab drivers had never heard of. Many of them felt it was just not good enough for them. The fact they were being taught by, or were working with, some of the world's best was nothing when set beside the — what would they call it? — *suburban* ambiance of Clare Hall.

Second example. One of my later graduate students was a woman more advanced in years than me, whose background was lower-middle class/working-class Northern Irish Protestant. When I accepted her I advised her to join Clare Hall, because they do such an excellent job with graduate students, especially the mature ones. After a few months she came to my office and told me that she'd decided to move to Pembroke College, where the Senior Tutor was inclined to accept her. Asked why she felt she had to leave Clare Hall she initially said that it was because one of the visiting fellows had made a pass at her. When I advised her to make an official complaint she tried to swat me off with a few improvised implausibles till eventually she said: "Well, actually Jim, my friends would expect me to be at a proper old college when they come to visit — not somewhere like Clare Hall." I said that was pure snobbery and that I would block the move, which, as Acting Senior Tutor at that time, I could. Clare Hall was good enough for the likes of Joseph Brodsky, Stefan Collini, Michael Green, Malcolm Longair, Keith O'Nions (for starters); but not for this woman.

Why do I feel compelled — as indeed I do — to include these sorry sagas in a book about bad psychology? They intensify the coldly judgemental tone I'm struggling to avoid, and there is nothing apparently relevant in them to the question of what is good and bad psychology. Having been interrogating myself, as the adrenaline breath of the first week of term eddies around me — that nicely postponed the moment when I have to write a cool sentence — I think the answer is this. These were intelligent people doing graduate work at one of the world's best universities and yet they were, in these cases, intensely concerned not about education but about social power, and with getting a short-cut to it by belonging to a certain kind of institution. The promise of a short-cut to social power is what lies at the fools-gold heart of king-the-ghosts-psychology.

Addiction to bad psychology is a part of something broader and deeper. All the varieties of meretricious baloney, be it existential psychology, positive psychology, transactional analysis, interpretive phenomenological analysis, and the like are short-cuts to social power, ways of saying: "I am not just a fellow human who is struggling along in life just like you. I am a psychologist who has special knowledge of these matters, so I will lay some wisdom on you." Why "short cut?" because it requires only the minimum of intelligence to understand the stuff. And my God the benefits! Instant respect from a certain kind of people. Maybe also the kind of people who think that if you are a member of a venerable college then you must be at least a little bit venerable yourself.

Connectionism

When I arrived at Cambridge two revolutions in psychological thinking were well underway, one essentially formal-conceptual and the other essentially empirical and springing from the ideas of Tom Bower (p.103 above). The "formal-conceptual" one was the beginning, or more accurately the intensification, of connectionist modelling. "Neural networks" had been around for some time (Piaget referred to a form of them in his work on logic), and it was the work of Geoffrey Hinton, Jeff Elman, David Rumelhart, Jay McClelland and others, and the latter two's *Parallel Distributed Programming* books, that really set the cat among the pigeons. Time to explain.

The way to frame this way of thinking is as the symmetrical opposite of Fodor's Platonic view of concept acquisition described above. The intuition here, recall, was that X cannot be learned unless you possess some representational format that represents the meaning of X prior to exposure to it, rather like saying the concept YELLOW cannot be learned unless you can already appreciate what all yellow things have in common. This representational format is a Language of Thought: it is symbolic.

What if you say instead that concept learning is *not* a matter of hypothesis-testing about the meaning of words — *hypotheses that come from some innate store of them*? What if you think it's more like the very simple processes of association that go on in animal learning, in the kind of learning, in fact, when, in the famous example, Pavlov's dog learned that a bell "means" food? Minimally, the argument runs, all a person has to do when learning the concept CAT is to associate the word "cat" with a set of perceptual features like "furry," "pointy ears," "tail," "four legged," "about the size of large handbag," "has whiskers." Why should it not be as conceptually simple as that? Yes, indeed, the correlation of features and symbols can be complex; but no innate format is required for it to work. This is a thoroughly empiricist way of thinking (an empiricist, recall, is somebody, like David Hume for example, who believes that all knowledge comes from perceptual experience). In fact, Hume's 18th Century notion of "the association of ideas" was not a million miles from the kind of process I am describing.

This way of thinking was underpinned by a general, formal (and so easy to mathematise) theory of conditioning of the Pavlovian or "classical" kind called the Rescorla-Wagner Rule. Applied in connectionism this is learning by *back propagation*. Let's turn to Rescorla-Wagner first.

The idea is that every stimulus an organism encounters has a particular "associative value" for the organism, and that when some surprising and significant event *follows* the stimulus this associative value increases. Accordingly, the sound of the bell in Pavlov's famous experiment had initially a low associative value until food-powder followed on from it. The same would be true if an electric shock had followed. Second, the amount of increase in associative value depends upon how surprising the subsequent event (food, shock) is. Thus, on the first trial, when the arrival of food is very surprising, there is a big increase in associative value, which gets smaller with each trial till the stimulus has accrued as much associative value as possible — the asymptote. While the Rescorla-Wagner Rule cannot explain all phenomena in classical conditioning, the kind of learning-by-prediction-error (surprisingness) idea that underlies it is immensely powerful and influential. It has been applied to the symptomatology of schizophrenia for example.[69] Indeed, it is essentially the "Delta Rule" that connectionist modellers use to enable networks, consisting only of units with

---

[69] Fletcher. P. and Frith, C. (2009) Perceiving is believing: A Bayesian approach to explaining the positive symptoms of schizophrenia. *Nature Neuroscience Reviews, 10*, 48-58.

activation levels and connections between them, to learn by back-propagation.[70]

I became an enthusiast for this; and there are many reasons why. Maybe part of me thought I should give empiricism a whirl so it could spin alongside all my other theoretical plates? Certainly, I was open to the radically empiricist message of connectionism. One local spur was Nick Mackintosh giving me, in my first term at Cambridge, a draft of a paper he was writing with Ian McLaren (then a graduate student) applying connectionist modelling to the phenomena of the peak shift (p. 50) and perceptual learning.[71] I wrote a long and enthusiastic commentary on it in which I found myself "whisking up a hopeful coda" of the kind I used to produce in my essays for Nick. In the coda I cheered on connectionism for being Humean and included a little Disney-level connectionist model (no maths) of the conservation task. *Apropos* conservation, probably the central reason connectionism interested developmental psychologists was that, obviously enough, it gives one a computational picture of development that is not

---

[70] What I have just described in only the most common form of connectionist modelling. There are others that are, unlike back-propagation, not dependent on feedback from errors. For example, there is Hebbian learning (after Donald Hebb) in which the fact of two associative units being activated together cements the connection between them. This has inspired connectionist theories of hypocampal function and rehabilitation — "what fires together, wires together."

[71] Perceptual learning is a phenomenon alluded to by William James in the context of wine tasting. In the context of animal learning: train the subject to discriminate between items in category A and in category B and they will become better at within-category discrimination (A1 versus A2; B1 versus B2 etc).

necessarily nativist (unlike Fodor's). Of course, learning is not the same thing as development; but it is a kind of *acquisition.*

I read quite a bit of the two *Parallel Distributed Processing* volumes and settled down to watch the impact of connectionism on development, never dreaming I would ever do any modelling of my own. Then all changed after my being re-acquainted with Kim Plunkett at a conference in the USA. He was about to move from Aarhus University in Denmark to a Lectureship in Oxford, having just published one of the landmark papers in developmental connectionism. A word about this paper to set the scene: one of the reasons given by nativists for thinking that rules override data in language development, for thinking that children know innately that their task is to figure out the abstract rules that govern the formation of words and phrases (not merely to "do statistics" on the input and draw inferences from that) is that children "over-regularise" words, especially verbs. For example, they may at first simply copy what they hear and say "brought," then later, having worked out that the rule for forming the past tense is "stem+ed," they will say "bringed," later abandoning this for "brought," having tagged it as an exception-to-the-rule — a "strong" verb. Along with Virginia Marchman, Kim had shown[72] that such U-shaped trajectories can be mimicked on a simple neural network, suggesting to some minds that we not only have no need for innate appreciation of linguistic rules, but no need of *rules.* The network did this, as well as predicting

---

[72]   Plunkett, K. and Marchman, V. (1991) in *Cognition, 38.,* p. 43

the existence of errors that children should make, which had yet to be reported — impressive indeed.

Kim spent his summers at the La Jolla campus of the University of Southern California at San Diego doing both research of the kind just described and helping to run, along with Jeff Elman and Liz Bates, a tutorial workshop on connectionist modelling for developmental psychologists. He invited me to joint it. It really was an invitation impossible to refuse: all expenses covered for 5 weeks. I *did* want a holiday in the sun, a cheap holiday in other people's luxury. There would be some teaching of me and I would have to do a project and return later in the summer to report on it at a plenary get-together for all the summer's attendees. It was a seductive prospect. I explained that I was a mathematical idiot who had never programmed a computer in his life, and that it was all I could manage to turn them on and off. Kim was having none of it, explaining that the La Jolla lab had developed a simulator program called 'tlearn' that enabled non-programmers to construct and run connectionist networks. You type in a few parameters and the program grinds away at the vector algebra. Even I could manage that.

It's difficult not to go over the top in praise for this La Jolla sojourn. Kim was a master teacher and a good companion, my tutorial partner Judith Goodman (a psycholinguist from the San Diego Psychology department) was a joy to work alongside … a Saturday being driven down to Coronado Beach to see the location of *Some Like it Hot*, evenings spent at *The Elephant Bar* being told I was like John Lennon till I opened my mouth… that kind of thing.

I had had the idea for my project before I arrived, and when Kim picked me up at the airport he told me in his usual upbeat way that yes of course that was do-able. It was based on a distinction which has obsessed me since my Kant tutorials with Harold Cox at Oxford (p.60): between changes in experience caused by our own actions and those caused by the world, thus marking off two different kinds of causality and being, for the Piagetian, the wedge that splits self from the physical world. The idea was to have an agent-like network predict the results of its own eye-movements or lack of them. Imagine there is a block before you and you launch an eye-movement of 10 degrees to the left. Then you will predict that your image of the block will move 10 degrees to the right; and if it does you conclude that the block did not really move. You launch no eye-movement and the block moves; then you conclude that it really did move. You launch an eye-movement 10 degrees to the left and the image does *not* move. In this case you (your brain rather) conclude that the block moved 10 degrees in the other direction, as the two must have cancelled each other out. Could a network learn this general principle?

The word "general" is important here. Connectionist networks can learn to map any set of inputs onto any set of outputs. You could give a network the task of mapping stations on the London underground to French cheeses, for example. The real challenge comes though when you train the network with a set of inputs (block positions, eye-movement direction and length) to a set of outputs (consequent visual images). If you train it with a *subset* of possible input-output pairings will the network be able to make the correct output/prediction *with inputs it has never "seen" before*? If it can then it has "gone beyond the information given:" it has *generalised*.

I could not get my net to generalise all the time I was in La Jolla. I would sometimes eat alone in the evenings scribbling the latest brain-waves, in the form of units (circles) and connections (lines with arrows), on *Taco Bell* paper napkins. The next morning I'd spread the napkin, stained with taco juice and still wet with *Corona*, beside the computer, try it that way, and watch it fail. I returned to Cambridge worried that my talk on the project a few weeks later in La Jolla would have the rhetorical force of banging a head against a brick wall. However, Ian McLaren (by this time a research fellow at Kings) saved the day. I told him about my generalisation problem over lunch in Kings, he told me what to do; and the network generalised. The solution involved having some of the input units only come on 0.5 rather than 1. In fact, I've forgotten the details, and have forgotten too the general conclusion I drew from it all, despite the fact that Kim and I tried to publish a paper on the lessons to be drawn for development. What I have not forgotten, though, is the immense generosity shown to me by what I think of as the back-room-boffins of connectionism (boffins with waist-length hair quite often) after I gave my report on the project back in La Jolla. They could see I had been struggling with a issue that meant a lot to me, and were interested in the solution. While I had misgivings about the "connectionist club" that Liz Bates seemed to be building around her, about the either-for-us-or-against-us ethos this fostered, this was a happy period of my life. Thanks to Kim.

Violation of expectation

Now to consider the second revolution. You may recall that Tom Bower had questioned Piaget's assumption that what an infant knows should be assessed in terms of what she can do. If we adopt this view, babies seem to know hardly anything about the physical and social worlds. If like Bower, however, we arrange things in order to see what surprises (note: no Recorla-Wagner relevance here!) them, then there seems to be quite a lot of knowledge in there. Accordingly, if we are interested in whether babies who cannot search for completely-occluded objects do, after all, know there is a hidden object present we might remove the occluder to reveal *no* object: that should be surprising if they thought there was one there but could do nothing about it.

You may also recall that Bower had used heart-rate drop as his measure of surprise, and that this was an insensitive measure. The revolution I am talking about came about through the use of a much more sensitive measure of surprise, namely, *looking-time*. Show a baby an object, and if it is moderately complex she will attend to it. After time, she will get bored and start to look away. If the stimulus is then changed, however, she may well look at it for longer periods, her interest renewed; and if she does then she must have *detected* the change. This is a very powerful way of finding out what babies can see. Indeed, it is also a powerful way of finding out what babies know about the continuing existence of objects they *cannot* currently see. Knowing that things are there despite our not perceiving them is about as fundamental as knowledge gets. As we saw much earlier, Piaget called it object permanence, assessing its development in terms of babies' ability to search for things they want, arguing that it is not complete until 18 months of age.

We can run very simple experiments modelled on the original Bower ones. We can, as we have seen, have a ball roll behind a screen then remove the screen. In one case there's the ball again; and in another case there's no ball. So will the babies look longer at the anomalous no-ball outcome *because it was not what they expected*? If they did expect to see the ball again then one might say they knew it was invisibly there even if they were unable to reach for it.

While this particular experiment was not done using increased looking time as the measure of surprise many other more ingenious ones were, the most well-known of which is Renée Baillargeon's so-called "drawbridge" experiment. In this, babies of 4 months of age — babies who were a full 4 months away from being able to search for things when they are fully occluded — watch a board swivel on a hinge towards and away from them for the full 180^0 until they grow tired of seeing it and start to look away. They then see a yellow wooden block (they have handled this and experienced its solidity) placed behind the board in its path, so that one would expect it to impede the backwards movement of the board, stalling it before the completion of the 180^0 arc. Note that as the board moves backward the block is rendered invisible. In one condition, this is indeed what happens: the board's backwards swing is stalled at 112^0. In the other condition, by contrast, the board travels back as usual through 180^0, as if the block were no longer there. Babies of 4 months of age look longer in this latter condition. What makes this so remarkable is that the 180^0 swing, which they had originally grown bored with, is now surprising them. If they were surprised at the outcome, then they must have "mentally represented" the block as being there at the time of the upward swing. So they must have had a kind of object permanence: knowledge that cannot be acted on.

On a similar theme, Elizabeth Spelke showed, among other things, that babies of 2-and-a-half months are surprised when a travelling ball "must have" passed through a wall behind a screen when the screen is removed. More precisely, they are more surprised than when, on removal of the screen, the wall *has* impeded the ball. For Spelke, this implies an innate appreciation of the solidity of objects, which is, for her, one component of an innate system of "naïve physics."

There was at that time, and still is, an awful lot of work of this dishabituation (or "violation-of-expectation" - VOE) kind, applying both to babies' knowledge of objects and to their causal interactions and to people and their behaviour — their intentions, preferences, the rationality of their actions (taking short cuts when possible), their attention, and to all the things that psychologists used to think were late-developing, because they depended upon years of social interaction. Needless to say, some of the results can be questioned; though the vast majority are rock-hard methodologically. And needless to say, there are indeed foundational arguments against the very idea of reading off infants' knowledge from what surprises them; but, for my money, none of them go through. In fact I think this is wonderful work. If anybody says to me: "OK, so what have developmental psychologists actually *discovered* in the last 50 years?" I'll tell them about this work.

When this work emerged I was a sceptic. It was not that I was instinctively against nativism, rather it was because I was a kind of psychological pragmatist. Not a philosophical pragmatist, a follower of William James, C.S. Peirce and Co, who held that truth reduces to the issue of what works — to its "cash value" for action. I was a psychological pragmatist, who roots the acquisition of knowledge in agency. In short, I agreed with Piaget that knowledge has to grow out of action and should be assessed in terms of what children can do, not in terms of how they *react to* events.

Agency: the role of writing this book in my mental development

In my previous two year-long sabbaticals I had written books, and did not think that this one (1993-94) should be an exception. What's more, I thought I had something strong to say, something about the conditions that have to be fulfilled if we are to acquire knowledge of things and thoughts. The book that emerged was *Agency: Its Role in Mental Development* (1996). In fact, this was no intellectual lightning-strike for me. It was the working out of a long-standing obsession, standing since — here we go again — my tutorials on Kant with Harold Cox. To anticipate, while I still think it's a good book, it is only good because I gave a certain line of thought a good run for its money. In fact it fails in its main purpose, for reasons that will emerge. Skimming through it now is like watching a man in well-tailored clothes and carefully sculpted hair trying to levitate.

With regard to the "long-standing obsession" readers might like to check back to what I said about the "Kant-Piaget axis" on page 59. In discussing causation, Kant distinguished between two kinds of dynamic experiences we can have: those that are within our power and reversible (like visually scanning a room); and those that are outside our power and irreversible (seeing a cat cross our path). This is a laughably un-Kantian way of putting it, but as we gain control over our eye and head movements we gradually becomes aware of the limits to our freedom to determine our own experiences. There is freedom — I can look at this then this and back — while there is correlative constraint: if I look over there I have absolutely no choice but to see an undergraduate in a red pullover leaving the lecture. Indeed, one can see the distinction as the thin end of the wedge that divides self from physical world: I choose what to see when I can, that is my contribution; and the world imposes experiences on me willy-nilly.

Reversibility is the hallmark of this kind of action. However, only some actions are reversible in principle: most clearly those with an attentional character (where nothing is touched). Try to reverse jumping into a swimming pool or punching a cushion. As I said a much earlier, reversibility was, for Piaget, the mark of "thought" as compared to "perception." In any event, this will be your position if you believe thinking is like attending, rather than like representing, as pragmatists do (as a schoolboy Piaget wrote an essay called "Sketch for a Neo-Pragmatism").

As for perception, he seemed to mean the passive receipt of light-rays, our being caused to see this or that.

I was happy to ally myself with Piaget and took to referring to my views as "piagetian" (little p) in talks and papers (I got the idea from seeing "marxian" and "marxist" in the *New Statesman*). I was also happy to spell out the implications of the Kant-derived position for the development of object permanence. What, then, are the implications? On the Kant-Piaget axis, there is a sense in which the exercise of agency, meaning in this case changing your perceptual inputs at will, enables one to "construct" — Piaget called one of his major books *The Child's Construction of Reality* — a category of data that are refractory, that resist our attempts at control, that lie "beyond" action. These data — objects — are agency-independent: we are caused to experience them, because they are mind-independent. So to know that there is an object "out there," let alone one currently occluded, must depend upon infants being at-least-moderately-skilled agents; and small babies are not. What's more, if a baby does not reach for an object she *wants* that is currently occluded and *she has the motor skill to search* then there can be no sense in which she knows it is there — on this view. For example, if a baby of 7 months (a month before they reach for completely occluded objects) sees the chocolate raisin that she wants very much put underneath a handkerchief so that it's no longer visible and she has the motor skill to search, *but she does not* then it simply make no sense to say she "has" object permanence based on data of the Baillargeon and Spelke kind. For that pragmatist, knowledge that you don't know how to act on is not knowledge

at all. OK, she may show surprise in the experiments by
Baillargeon and Spelke just described, but this surprise must be
due to something other than knowledge of the mind-
independence of the external world.

I have to admit to struggling nowadays to articulate this
view of object permanence because I no longer believe it. As I
type the sentences I can see lacunae looming. In the mid-'90s,
though, I was full of passionate conviction, writing papers with
titles like "At Two with Nature" (a Woody Allen crack about an
urban Jew in the countryside), arguing for the view that self-
world dualism *must* depend upon agency. I am not saying that
this view has no merit in it at all — it does have some. But, the
attempt to downgrade the results of Baillargeon, Spelke and
others was wrongheaded, and the idea that the exercise of
agency alone can bootstrap you up to a "*concept* of an
object" (the other Piagetian term for object permanence) was
doomed, as was the assumption that agency is sufficient to
divide self from physical world. I'll come to the first two
problems in a while, and here's a note about the last one. I
edited a collection for Blackwell shortly before I left Liverpool
called *Philosophical Perspectives on Developmental
Psychology* in which my old philosophy tutor Jim Hopkins (p.
60) had a chapter. It was a brilliant piece which reviewers
tended to say was the best in the book. Despite finding some of
the material on Melanie Klein a bit hard to swallow (a field-day
phrase for Kleinians) I was entirely convinced by his argument
that unless infants begin with *some* recognition that certain
stimuli are "from the outside" (e.g., looming faces) and that
some are "from the inside" (e.g., hunger pangs) then no amount

of Piagetian action can divorce self from world. My point being that I knew this, and knew in my heart that I was pushing the envelope beyond my reach; but I went on regardless.

In short, I wrote the book with the kind of fanciful focus that I would now associate with king-of-the-ghosts psychology. I was not merely philosophically convinced about my agency thesis — there was much use of Schopenhauer in the book: the world being "will" as well as "representation[73]": I was in the grip of a vision of What Humans are Fundamentally Like. One of my papers (in a book edited by Ray Tallis) had been called "Im Anfang war die Tat" (Goethe's *Faust*: in the beginning was the deed) and countless times this bit of easy resonance appeared on the slides of my talks. As I said earlier, the not-so-resonant phrase "Never Mind the Bollocks, it's the Executive Functions" cropped up in one of the gonzo-of the-imagination conference sketches I used to write for the BPS Developmental Section Newsletter.

I remember typing furiously away at the book on one of those early, periscope-like Apple-Macs one sunny afternoon on June the 6th 1994 in Bristol as my father was dying in the next room. I was so riveted to the book, so convinced I had something hot to say. And all this fuss, when much of the time I was doing no more than looking for loopholes in infancy experiments. What do I mean by this last sentence? Let us return to the dishabituation research on object permanence. I

---

[73] Schopenhauer argued that we know everything representationally except facts about our willing: our epistemic relation to our volitional states is not a representational one. Philosophers would call this "immediate" (i.e., unmediated) knowledge. The title of his great work was *Die Welt als Wille und Vorstellung*.

had to come up with ways of interpreting the results of the work by Spelke, Baillargeon and others as not being about object permanence at all (in fact this followed one of my inglorious traditions, as I had been looking for interpretive loopholes within the Tom Bower work in my 1978 book). I argued that these experiments showed not object permanence, but "representation permanence." The idea here was that the infants kept the representations of the occluded objects alive in their minds (or mind-brains) with no accompanying belief as to their being representations of something in the external spatial world of solid stuff. Rather as we might keep Michelle Pfeiffer in mind when she hides in a cupboard in a movie, without thinking she is actually in the world now before us. We would never reach for her, even if we were that near to the screen. In fact, this is far from being a silly idea in itself. Andy Meltzoff[74] (p.109) has argued for something similar with his idea of "representational persistence." Where Meltzoff was fielding the idea as a possible explanation of the developmental gap between what looking-time experiments reveal about infant capacities and what infants actually do, I was, by contrast, launching a doomed defence of the Piagetian idea that activity *alone* can bootstrap a child from being somebody who knows nothing about the mind-independent existence of physical objects to somebody who can conceptualise their mind-independent existence.

---

[74] Meltzoff, A. and Moore, K. (1998) Object representation, identity, and the paradox of early permanence. *Infant behaviour and Development, 21,* 201-235.

The word "conception" is important here. My group used to have lab meetings in those days, when one of us would give a talk for critiquing by the rest. When it was my turn, I presented an early and fairly naïve draft of my "At Two with Nature" paper, in which I attempted the ten-mile leap from action-experience to conception, arguing that if an infant's understanding of how her actions do and do not affect her perceptions then she has the grounding for "the object concept." At that time one of my graduate students was Teresa McCormack; and she was having none of it. Teresa was unencumbered by deference and almost shouted: "But you are talking about *conception*!" A visitor to the lab commented after, that this proved how "comfortable" they felt with me. Well ...

Concepts are what we think with. They are more than and different from knowing what leads to what and parcelling up the perceived world up into bundles: both things that connectionist modelling does so well. So, predictably, in the book there were many words said in favour of connectionism. In fact, I never really gave any serious thought to the limitations of connectionist theory as a theory of *thought*. The other day a colleague of mine said that the connectionist project had failed. Not really. It succeeds brilliantly in modelling those processes that are indeed associative (like learning grammatical gender, learning the six forms of the definite pronoun in German,[75] modelling the interactions between the hippocampus, the medial parietal and the pre-frontal cortex in

---

[75] MacWhinney et al (1989) Language learning: cues or rules. *Journal of Memory and Language, 28*, p. 255

episodic memory [76]), but if your interest is in conceptualisation — in the ability to think about things "without the mind[77]" and about the mind itself — then you had better look elsewhere, somewhere symbolic. In fact, writing the book and constantly finding myself thinking, "Why are you making life so difficult for yourself?" turned me, by a gradual process, into a nativist, and more specifically into a Fodorian. Jerry Fodor wrote around this time (original emphasis).[78]

> In linguistics and elsewhere it invariably turns out that there's more in the content of our concepts than there is in the experiences that prompt us to form them.[...]The empiricist programme was in place for several hundred years, not just in psychology but also — indeed especially —in epistemology and the philosophy of science, where a lot of clever people wasted a lot of time trying to reduce "theoretical" concepts (like TABLE) to "observation" concepts (like RED and SQUARE). There were in the course of those centuries *no successes at all*; literally *none*; which is to say *not one*. [...] So it looked, until just recently, that the argument between empiricism and rationalism had been put to rest. The connectionists have revived it ..."

---

[76] Discussed in Burgess, N., Becker, S., King, J. A. and O'Keefe, J. (2001) Memory for events and their spatial context: models and experiments. *Proceedings of the Royal Society of London, B, 356*, 1-11.

[77] In his paper "Things without the mind" Gareth Evans discusses what is involved conceptually in taking an object to be mind-independent. This is to be found in his collection *Philosophical Subjects* (Clarendon Press).

[78] From his 1998 review of Elman et al's *Re-thinking Innateness* in his collection *In a Critical Condition*. (MIT Press).

Autism: exercising a hobby horse then hobbling home

There was, though, a less ambitious and more empirically tractable way of thinking about the "role of agency in mental development" — though, conveniently for myself, I did not mark the difference in the book. It kept my research going for the remainder of the decade, until I lost faith in it. In a sense it was a harking back to the kind of approach I repudiated earlier in the context of conservation and other Piagetian tasks: the idea that children are not really failing certain tests because they lack the concepts. They are failing them for extraneous reasons. These extraneous reasons were the familiar ones of executive dysfunction (see the Windows Task; p.59 above). It barely crossed my mind in those days that if I was arguing that they had the concept — a concept of mind in this case — *already* then I was heading for nativism whether I liked it or not. In fact, my interest during this period was not so much in the normal course of cognitive development, but in autism.

To say the least, autism is a multifaceted phenomenon and there has been a long history of autism researchers focusing on their favoured facet. They are like the blind men in the Indian fable each of whom thinks in turn, that an elephant is a snake, wall or tree depending on whether they touch the trunk, belly, or leg. The autism researchers are fully-sighted but blinkered. In my case, I had come to the view (a view based on a king-of-the-ghostian determination to see the root of all mentality in action) that the impairments that individuals with autism showed in so-called mentalising were rooted in the early (12- to 18 months) failure to control experience…and here we are back again with Kant's Second Analogy (pp.204-5, above). If a toddler's perceptual experiences change and she does not know whether the changes were caused by her or by the world, then how could she ever be in a position to differentiate subjective from objective experience? Experience would be chaotic and "selfless." Such a child may indeed have some kind of innate module for mentalising. However, this could never properly be put to use. How — the argument ran — can you acquire a theory of mind unless you have a coherently experiencing mind of which it is to be a theory, with the implication being that a child would be unable to cognise the mental states of others without some secure sense of her own mental states. What's more, if experience became chaotic in this way would such a child not try to impose order by the obsessive repetition of actions (e.g., repeatedly twirling objects) — as children with autism indeed do?

My thought was that what "goes wrong" in the brain of the child who develops autism is the efference-copying mechanism, meaning the monitoring of any launched action to ensure that experiential changes caused by that action "will come as no surprise."[79] At roughly the same time Chris Frith[80] was developing a theory of schizophrenia that bears comparison with this idea. He argued that autism and

---

[79] The notion of efference copying originates with Ebbinghaus: when a motor act is launched by the brain a copy of the command is made (an efference copy) in order that the perceptual result of the action can be compared against the expected prediction, based on this. It has been called a forward model. If there is discrepancy between prediction and outcome there is surprise. There are clear similarities to "feed-forward" connectionist models here and to the Rescorla-Wagner Rule.

[80] See his *Cognitive Neuropsychology of Schizophrenia* (The Psychology Press)

schizophrenia have in common impairments in self-monitoring. I too argued this though in mirror image, saying that in autism efference-copying goes array in toddlerhood causing a theory of mind to fail to develop, while in schizophrenia it goes wrong in adulthood or late adolescence causing a derangement of theory of mind. Chris Frith's position, by contrast, was that self-monitoring depends on a sense of self, which depends upon a theory of mind, and so the monitoring deficits in schizophrenia that lead, on his theory, to auditory hallucinations and delusions of control are rooted in theory-of-mind deficits.[81]

I did not, however, try to test my position in a truly developmental way by testing children who were at risk from developing autism, in the expectation that these children would initially show impairments in self-control before showing social impairments in joint-attention, gesture, eye-contact, and so forth. Instead I launched, thanks to generous support from the Wellcome Trust, what felt like a campaign to discover the forms of executive functioning that are unique to autism. I also wanted to show — somewhat illogically, given that I had never *denied* that there are mentalising problems in autism — that autistic failure on mentalising tasks is really an executive failure in many cases.

I did some good work in this era, in spite of my theoretical rigidity and the fact that keeping your fingers crossed that the autistic group will perform significantly worse than the

---

[81] For recent developments in Frith's thinking see: Fletcher. P. and Frith, C. (2009) Perceiving is believing: A Bayesian approach to explaining the positive symptoms of schizophrenia. *Nature Neuroscience Reviews, 10*, 48-58 .

mentally-handicapped control group (not at all the same thing as "showing an impairment"!) is not the most exciting way to do research. It was a happy research era. This was due in part to my "allies" and co-workers. In the first category I place the American autism researchers Sally Ozonoff and Bruce Pennington, who, far from treating me as a Johnny-come-lately to the executive-autism game were richly supportive (two of the nicest people I have met in my career). In the latter category I was lucky to have Chris Jarrold (preceding Rebecca Saltmarsh and Elisabeth Hill) as the post-doctoral worker on the Wellcome grant. He had his own good ideas, and was sensitive in his delivery of various reality checks to me.

It was also a happy time personally. I met my second wife, Sally Barrett-Williams, on a blind date in London arranged by Annette Karmiloff-Smith[82] in 1994. We married the following year. Sally was brilliant, beautiful, and exciting. Her second home was an ex-presbytery in Picardy; and soon we shared our first home in London. The trouble was, though, that both the marriage and the research programme had that familiar thing in this narrative — built-in obsolescence. The marriage, because whatever it was that Sally and I had together was destined to atrophy within two or three years. I moved back to Cambridge and we divorced in 1998. As for the research, I ended up showing at least as much about the *intact* executive abilities in autism as about the impaired ones. Centrally, our studies of action-monitoring in autism often showed no evidence of

---

[82] Annette Karmiloff-Smith (1938-2016) was a major figure in developmental psychology, with a unique intellectual profile — from work with Piaget in Geneva, through large- scale theorising about cognitive change, to her most recent research into developmental disorders, such as Williams Syndrome.

impairment. As I re-jigged the theory, prediction-failures kept popping up as in a game of Whack-a-Mole. I could have kept on re-jigging my position till it was utterly changed, but with my name still on it. In the end I simply lost interest.

It was not so much a matter of losing interest in autism as of slowly coming to realise, as the millennium ended, that this was not the way to do research. My theoretical position was a kind of conceptual "punt," a king-of-the-ghostian picture of human mentality that one could only set to empirical test with fingers crossed. I still stand by some of it, and believe to this day in many of the positions set out in my book *Agency* book; but the autism work lacked the essential scientific touchstones of modesty and realism. I dragged my bloodied carcass away from the field of autism and sat it down before my stereo with a bottle of wine and a packet of cheroots.

Getting to grips, or not, with later Chomsky

I was leading an unhealthy life as the new millennium began; and in the Spring of 2000 I had a stroke. Not a major stroke, but enough of one to ensure that I have to type these words now with my right hand only. It lead me to resign my Fellowship at my second college, Churchill; and I became college-less for 6 years.

I did not actually have a real research programme at this time, though some empirical work did get done— on observational learning for example. Taking stock, I asked myself what I was really interested in and what I really wanted to get to grips with. In both cases the answer was "language acquisition" — the growth of syntax in particular and the latest developments in Noam Chomsky's ideas about it, in particular to that. Oxford University Press gave me a contract to write a book in my 2000-2001 sabbatical year — *What is Language Development? — Empiricist, Rationalist, and Pragmatist Approaches to the Acquisition of Syntax.* The book did get written, and was published in 2004, its lateness due mainly to my stroke-induced typing problems.

Whilst thinking Chomsky is a great genius I also think that there is something odd about his claim that he is "doing science;" and this because one looks in vain for the modesty and realism I mentioned earlier. Everything about Chomsky simultaneously invites admiration and frustration. On the one hand it seems to be entirely justified for a linguist to say, based on his analysis of human grammatical competence, that it is impossible for a child to acquire language without innate knowledge of certain basic principles and operations; and indeed, to insist that theories of acquisition should be based on linguistic theory — not on some washy stuff about turn-taking and intersubjectivity. On the frustrating side, however, Chomsky is not only evasive about the empirical implications for how his abstract theories relate to real-time processing in the (his coining) mind-brain: he carries the evasion before him like a banner. He seems to think it's almost philistine to wonder whether the operations he describes are descriptions of real mental processes. In the early days when he spoke of "kernel" sentences, "deep-structure," and "transformational

complexity" it was relatively straightforward for
psycholinguists to test these ideas in the lab with people
reading and generating sentences. However, in the latest
incarnations of the theory, while the operations themselves are
unexcitingly intuitive the steps through which they are
instantiated reveal a Platonic homunculus who does what he
has to do constrained only by a kind of necessity (see
immediately below) unique to Chomsky.[83] How could one
apply these ideas to processing and development? The 1995
theory was called The Minimalist Program, but it is formally
maximalist — to the max. Many linguists and
psycholinguists[84] who were once deeply sympathetic to
Chomsky are now stern critics.

I did my best to set out Chomsky's Minimalist Program in
the book, to make it sound plausible to say that the structure of
the syntactic system is as it is through a kind of "necessity"
given the structure of the conceptual systems (the way we
think) and of the articulatory-perceptual systems (our
perceptual and vocal apparatuses). For Chomsky, syntax is
more like a snowflake than a giraffe's neck, thus alluding to the
fact that physical laws, not contingent evolution, give
snowflakes the form they have. Analogizing to syntax, there is
a similar kind of necessity at work. making syntactic form
"more like a snowflake than a giraffe's neck " – structural

[83] Howard Lasnik provides an accessible account of the minimalist program in: Lasnik, H. (2002) The minimalist program in syntax. *Trends in Cognitive Sciences, 6,* 432-437.

[84] For a piece by Steven Pinker and Ray Jackendoff critical of the implications of minimalism for language evolution see: Pinker, S. and Jackendoff, R. (2005) The faculty of language: What's special about it? *Cognition, 95(2):*201--236.

necessity, not contingent biological history. I transcribed and reproduced an interview Chomsky did for Radio 3 about language evolution in which he invited us to imagine early humans wandering the earth a million or so years ago thinking all the kinds of thoughts that we can think now, only for a "shower of cosmic rays" to implant a language acquisition devise into them (only a thought experiment!), though needing the right kind of "interface" with the external (conceptual and articulatory-perceptual systems). And I sweated blood getting to grips with the technicalities of the Minimalist Program.

I never thought that I was not justified in bothering with all this, because empiricist (i.e., connectionist) and pragmatist (i.e., Michael Tomasello's view that grammar is learned without innate preparation of a specifically linguistic kind) were having too good a run for their money (I heard a linguistics undergraduate phoning in to Jonathan Ross's radio show one Saturday tell the audience not to bother with Chomsky as "Mike Tomasello's the man"). I finished the book feeling I had not fully convinced even myself. Right now I feel we need linguist/psychologists who do the same *kind* of thing as Chomsky does while acknowledging the centrality of semantic structure, and who are not afraid to hack away the eccentricities from the theory and carve out some plausible mechanisms that have a life off the page.

In fact, I have to say that placing Chomskyan theory in a book about the ghostly over-reaching of psychology, makes one view the work as ghostly itself. There is an easy comparison with Freud. Here is a charismatic thinker with absolute self-confidence, whose followers tack and twist with his every change of mind, creating not a set of hypotheses, but a hermeneutic circle insulated against empirical bruising.

Around the time of writing the book I met Maria Angeles Gallego, a linguist of a more down-to-earth variety. She was a post-doc working on Judeo-Arabic (Arabic used by Jews with some differentiating features including the use of the Hebrew alphabet in writing). We began a relationship, which did not survive her move back to Madrid; and we continue, and will continue, as close friends. I have a great debt of gratitude to Marigel. She helped to cure me of the drinking habits that continued after the stroke, and she showed me a scholar at work. To do the kind of work she does one must have a grasp of mind-boggling detail, a knowledge of subtle linguistic nuances and a secure knowledge of Mediterranean history. One must at once master and remember the little local principles and have a broad historical sense.

When I attended a seminar she gave in her faculty I witnessed the stark contrast between the scholarly seminar and the kind we had in our department. Notably, the Zangwill Club. Although Marigel was "only" a postdoc, the big room was packed with people ranging from major historians such as David Abulafia to junior philologists. And when the questions started the atmosphere was collegial, sharing various expertises towards a common goal. Over at the Zangwill Club, though, it was so often a matter of coming up with killer questions, a matter of look-at-me.

All this goes along with another contrast: where scholars of this kind march onward in tandem, psychologists at Marigel's then junior level see themselves as surfing a wave of brilliance, with their compulsive downloading of the latest papers, endless collaborations on fashionable paradigms; and their narrowness.

The above is perhaps unfair and over-stated, and yet it was how I thought then. I find it hard to shake the thinking of it now.

Back from the brink… to episodic memory

At this period I was contemplating early retirement. What was the point of being an academic psychologist if I was only doing a dribble of research, if I had no intellectual "horse" (to re-encounter Freud's expression), and if teaching gave me (and the students) little satisfaction? I did not do this, thank goodness, and instead became interested in the development of episodic memory; and this almost by accident. I climbed onto a horse.

One lunchtime I went along to a talk by my colleague Tony Dickinson about episodic memory in birds — scrub jays. This was a provocative enough topic, because episodic memory would seem to be something uniquely human. It means the conscious, indeed re-experiential, recollection of personal events in one's life, whether 50 years or 50 seconds ago. Indeed, for reasons that would take a long time to articulate, episodic memory must be bound up with a sense of self. Tony's argument now is so well known within cognitive psychology that it could almost be set to music. It is one that depends upon a provocative interpretation of the original definition of episodic memory by the coiner of the term Endel Tulving: "Episodic memory receives and stores information about temporally dated episodes or events, and temporal-spatial relations among these events." Now this definition really is minimalist, though in the traditional sense, not the Chomskyan one touched on above. Tony's argument was that what the definition boils down to is the ability to remember what happened, where, and when. "What" is a semantic something: a kind of object say; "Where" is where the object was located; and "When" is how long ago from the present time the locating was done. Scrub jays seem to have this kind of What-When-Where, or WWW, memory. The studies that Tony went on to describe had not been run by him, but by his collaborator Nicola (Nicky) Clayton. Born in Blackpool, Nicky was at that time working at the University of California at Davis, after a period at Oxford.

Scrub jays are food-caching birds, which have a prodigious memory for where their food had been cached; and they are not the only animal to have this capacity. The further question is whether they can "bind" (in the jargon) recall of where the food was cached to recall of what kind of food was cached and how long ago it was cached. They can, in the following sense. The "What" is variety of food: either peanuts, which the jays like but would not die for, and the "wax worms" (moth larvae), which they love. They strongly prefer the wax worms, but will settle for peanuts. The "Where" is one of two places, say A and B, in which they cached one of the foods or another. The "When" is how long ago they were cached. In all this, one crucial fact is that the peanuts stay fresh for a long time and the wax worms soon die and become rotten and unpalatable. Given all this, let's say a bird caches peanuts in place A and wax worms in place B and then goes away for a short time. The "rational" thing to do — for a bird that can bind WWW — is to go to B, where the wax worms will be fresh. However, if it had gone away for a long time a WWW-binder would go to A, because the food has become inedible at B.

Episodic memory? Tony and Nicky hedged on this. They called what the jays could do "episodic-like" memory, because one cannot interrogate the animals about their experiences. This struck me as an odd position then, and still does, given that speech does not give us direct access to the speaker's conscious states; indeed, what others *do* may speak louder. In any event, I was fascinated by this work; though fascinated too by how vociferously dismissive were some of the voices from the audience —especially Ian McLaren's (a Lecturer by then). In fact, at that time — around 2003 — I did not quite know where I stood on the issue of bird memory. I did, though, know the work had strong, but not yet clear, relevance to human development. Minimal tests of something that goes to the heart of human mental life are catnip to a developmental psychologist.

My first thought was to go away and run an experiment on "event versus location memory" in toddlers. I won't bore you with the details. Essentially, the study involved the children seeing somebody taking a toy from a box and leaving a second box with a toy still in it. When they come back and go to the untouched second box are they recalling an event (the removal) or the remaining location? A second experiment told us it was the location that they recalled. It was a neat study that actually told us rather little about early event memory, but it was a start and we got it into a good journal.

A year or so later, when Nicky took up a Lectureship in our department and was very keen to collaborate with me on some aspect of child episodic memory, I dragged my feet. This was not because there were no worthy things one could do using the caching/devaluing-over-time paradigm. I did them (hot cupboards that melt chocolate for instance). I was reluctant, because I had no particular theoretical slant on all this — no real ideas. We collaborated via graduate students on other topics, but it was not until Nicky persuaded me to co-author a paper with her on animal and child episodic memory that I got my theoretical boots on. I took the central readings away with me to Spain to see Marigel, and during the course of this trip came to realise why I was uncomfortable with the Clayton-Dickinson view of episodic memory.

Yes, the least you can say about episodic memory is that it is spatiotemporal. The problem was that the temporal element in the Clayton-Dickinson position seemed wrong to me — and neither did it map on to the Tulving quote particularly well. Remember that, for Clayton-Dickinson, the When in WWW means how long ago (was the caching done). In the first place, it struck me that the knowledge of how far back in the past the re-experienced episode took place is not relevant to the episodic character of the memory. While the how-long-ago is something we may know, it seems more like a semantic add-on.

So why then is episodic memory spatiotemporal? Because perceptual *experience* is spatiotemporal and, although episodic memory is not like a flashback, it has an ineluctably re-experiential character. At this point Kant came into my work again. Not the Kant of the Second Analogy, but the Kant of an earlier section of the *Critique* (the Transcendental Aesthetic), in which he famously argued that space and time are "a priori." He did not mean by this that knowledge of space and time is innate. He meant that all perceptual experience has a spatial and a temporal character. Is this true of purely *auditory* experience? (Is purely auditory experience spatial too? — a philosopher once asked me. I have no idea). I will not give a careful exposition here and I will just appeal to intuition. Imagine that somebody is experiencing a football and a banana. Spatially she'll see them in certain spatial relations to her (e.g., football near on her left and banana in the distance right above her head). Temporally, she'll see them appearing at the same time or successively — ball then banana, banana then ball. So this is a central point: for Kant — and surely he was right — the temporal character of perceptual experience, and thus of perceptual *re*-experience, is *simultaneity and succession*. It is not how-long-ago.

How to test this idea? As it turned out, I had already tested it — with Jonathan Davies, then my excellent graduate student (now a medic). We had tested WWW memory in children by using the technique of deferred imitation (pioneered by Piaget) which means showing children a novel action (or actions) on a novel object that produces an interesting outcome and then inviting them to try to reproduce this some time after (in our case, a day after). The apparatus was a schematic boat with levers on the left and right-hand side. The boat had "broken down" and what had to be done to get it going again was to pump the lever on the left – and afterwards lift and depress the lever on the right. Here the "What" was type of action, Where was left-right, *and "When" was the order of the actions.*

Now, for the first time in a long time, I felt I had something to say and do. The saying was a theoretical paper on the notion of minimalist episodic memory: (a) saying a proper account of WWW memory requires Kant on the spatiotemporal in experience; (b) saying Tulving (and Josef Perner too) are right to emphasise how minimal episodic memory falls far short of the richly self-knowing nature of episodic memory after 5 years or so; (c) describing the lessons to be learned from the study with Jonathan; (d) saying why WWW binding should be all-of-a–piece rather than atomistic; (e) showing how data from the deferred imitation task supported (d) in-so-far as no children who chose the correct actions and bound the correct actions to the correct side got the *order* wrong. Their memory had a holistic character — as does experience. As I wanted to say a lot about Kant in the paper (eventually published in the journal *Mind and Language*) I brought in somebody I'd known since my Clare Hall days — Bob Hanna from Colorado, an expert on Kant. I was lucky to have had two good people to work with at this time — Jonathon and Bob.

What I had to do, of course, was to gain funding to run more and tighter experiments and nail the matter down. Thanks to the Leverhulme Trust I managed this. They gave me one big grant to study the development of the early, minimal kind of episodic memory in pre-school children and the later form that depends on certain forms of conceptual development having taken place (theory of mind is central in the latter case). As well as a second grant to look at pre-experiential thinking ("episodic foresight"), on which I worked until retirement and slightly beyond.

You would think I had learned my lesson with Rita Hawksmoor (p.171). I had not, and the Leverhulme work was nearly still-born, due to an hilariously bad appointment as post-doctoral research associate. She was a Greek lady, who had seemed clever and easy-going at interview, but after a month of her I actually began to wonder if she had stolen the identity of the person she claimed to be: with the first-class degree and a Ph.D. in children's episodic memory with one of the memory legends at UCL. Was she even Greek at all? I seriously considered trying to introduce her to a friend from Queens' (my new college, more of which later) who really was Greek. She looked and sounded Russian ("Schizotypy?" The psychologist readers will be thinking). Anyway, it all ended well, with the appointment of Patrick (Pat) Burns to replace her. Not since the days of Chris Jarrold have I enjoyed working with somebody so much.

I'm glad the last phase of my career has been in the field of episodic memory. Some of the best brains in developmental psychology (e.g., Josef Perner, Teresa McCormack) and philosophy (e.g., John Campbell, Christoph Hoerl) work in it, and it forces one to think about the central matter of psychology: consciousness. The psychology of consciousness is almost a popular topic now, since the rise of neuro-imagining. But this latter has tended: (a) to be focussed on awareness, considered as a kind of threshold, rather than consciousness itself; and (b) to involve hubristic hints-cum-claims about solving the mind-body problem/the problem of qualia.[85] Philosophers have failed, they hint, but now we have fMRI ... Developmental work, by contrast, brings one back to traditional metaphysical problems: the role in consciousness of spatial processing, of bodily and self-awareness, of the necessity or otherwise for being a concept-user, and of the unity of the perceptual field (see WWW binding above).

The last thing I intended by the previous couple of sentences is that work like this should be conducted in isolation from neuroscience. The opposite is the case; and this is another argument for the fecundity of developmental work on episodic memory. It is a central fact that the brain structure most clearly implicated in (at least primitive forms of) episodic memory is the hippocampus; and this is the area that also seems to process absolute or allocentric (what's near what in a layout) as opposed to egocentric (or point-of-view) space. In my first year in Cambridge I had attended a workshop in Kings on spatial understanding at which John O'Keefe from UCL gave a paper on how the rat hippocampus processes space. In the edited book, which emerged from the meeting, he had a chapter called "Kant and the Seahorse" ("hippocampus" is from the Greek for seahorse) in which he argued for a position I thought was wrong then, and continued to think was wrong till about 2014: that the kind of space that Kant had in mind (or should have had in mind) in his "a priori of space and time" was

---

[85] "Qualia" is the plural of the Greek work *quale*, meaning the particular quality that something has. Seeing red, feeling pain, being happy have particular "what-it-is-essentially-like-nesses." Behaviouristically inclined philosophers like Dennett expend a lot of energy arguing against the very idea of qualia.

allocentric space (e.g., facts about the mind-independent, features of the spatial world like "the chair is by the window," as opposed to "the chair is on my left" – egocentric. Surely — I thought — the kind of space that is implicated in perceptual experience is egocentric space, space from a point of view, given that experience has to be from a point of view.

When Pat Burns and I ran our first deferred-imitation study with 2 to 3-year olds, in which we compared allocentric with egocentric information, we found that it was only in the *allocentric* condition that What-When-Where recall had the kind of holistic character (in which recall of a part would tend to mean recall of whole – rarely getting two from the three, for example) that would seem to be the hallmark of re-experiential memory. I had predicted that we would find this only in the egocentric condition. When you actually think about it, though, this should not be surprising, and not because of what we know about hippocampal function. A point of view is a point of view of *something* — of some layout — and if you cannot think about the inherent allocentric character of the layout then how can you experience it as relative to your own point of view?[86]

---

[86] An excerpt from Burns P, Russell, C. and Russell, J.'s "Pre-school children's proto-episodic memory assessed by deferred imitation." Published in the journal *Memory*, in 2015 "...imagine a visitor to London standing looking down Kensington Road with the Albert Hall on her left and the Albert Memorial on her right. She episodically recalls this view some time later. One object is on her left and one is on her right, but within her episodic recollection of standing there these egocentric relations are taken to be such because the Albert memorial is *in front of* the concert hall with her body between them. *The point-of-view is a function of where she was and what was before what.* So the paradox is resolved: recollection from an egocentric perspective can be grounded in allocentric coding, because "A on the left of B" in her experience and re-experience is known to be due to the fact   that her spatial position triangulated the two with B in front of A."

So John O'Keefe was right — the Nobel Prize winner was right (in my defence though, I would bet good money that egocentric space was what Kant had in mind[87]).

Somewhere in the brain, if not in the hippocampus, this point-of-viewness of episodic memory must be computed. This is likely to be the parietal region. This brings me to my daughter Charlotte (now a Senior Lecturer at Kings, London) and why she was a collaborator on our first Leverhulme grant. For reasons unknown to science, Charlotte and I became interested, quite independently, in the way in which episodic memory is perspectival. She carried this forward by doing imaging studies with intact subjects and by working with parietal patients (they have to say whether a video of their past experience was from their own view-point) and both of us did so in children (they have to say whether a video of an event from a certain point-of-view could have been their own view at the time).

Literature and psychology redux

Nicky Clayton is somebody to whom I feel gratitude. She did the work that provoked me and she forced me to come up with something fresh by suggesting the collaborative paper. But we are poles apart in our thinking about episodic memory. While

---

[87] Kant writes: "Considering the things which exist outside ourselves: it is only in so far as they stand in relation to ourselves that we have any cognition of them by means of our senses at all."

she talks of "mental time travel" (the conscious zooming from past to future while knowing we are in the present) in jays I see this as quite wrong, because if you are chary about ascribing conscious states to non-verbal creatures ("episodic-*like*" recall) then you'd better stay away from the term "mental time travel" as applied to animals. She would say her use of the term is a mere short-hand for a set of behaviours and that it comes complete with implicit caveats; to which I would say….well never mind. In any event, when we occasionally meet for a drink we stay away from the contentious stuff and just have a good gossip. It is easy to accentuate the positive with her.

There is indeed a deeper and wider difference between us — also Britishly avoided when we meet up: how we see the relation between science and the arts? For Nicky, there is a symbiotic relationship between the two: "Science and Dance" is one of her projects, while she's the "Scientific Advisor to the Rambert Ballet" (I recall Libby Purvis poking very gentle fun in her introduction to Nicky on *Midweek*: "A bit like being rear gunner for the National Theatre"). At TED talks and elsewhere there is much about 'the imagination' – a bran tub we can draw from both as scientists and as artists.

I say this now, because I have come to believe the exact opposite, rather late in my career; and because, more centrally, believing the opposite enables one to see the revenant King of the Ghosts plain. Recall that in my Oxford days, and indeed before, I had tried to write poems and stories, never getting anywhere. So as a kind of compensation mechanism I would over-write when writing psychology. All my psychology books, and some journal papers (where I could get away with it) were over-written to the point of being *belle-lettrist*, with Browning, George Eliot, and others crow-barred in (yes, *this* book is self-consciously written, with lots of arty flourishes. *Over*-written? Maybe, though I think not). As the years went on two things happened: I began to be able to write poems worthy of the name, and I began to relish the plain-ness of scientific prose, and the refreshingly un-poetic qualities of good prose in writers as diverse as Bertrand Russell, Richard Yates, and Charles Willeford. As I wrote more poems —95% of them failures— my view of scientific psychology sharpened.

Where is the imagination in all this? Of course you need imagination to do science, even to dream up an appropriate control group; and the practice of art may be quite unimaginative (photorealism?). In science, though, we are aiming at mind-independent truth (I imagine the social-relativists in the wings trying to hook me off the stage and sneering at what Rorty called, as I mentioned long ago, the phallocentic metaphor of depth). Science should be as ego-less as humanly possible, sober, and without any literary curlicues whatsoever. Experimental science teaches one to be humble before the facts. Psychology is hardly awash with this attitude.

I published my first poem in a magazine in 1999, my first collection came out in 2004, and at the time of writing I've published six books of poetry (collections, pamphlets, and a novella with poems), and have a new collection in the pipeline. The chapbooks tend towards the satirical, and I will describe the genesis of one of them later. The relevance of all this will shortly emerge.

How I learned the ghost was still thriving

In 2009 I met a French lady, Carole Radanne, who would eventually become my third wife. We had planned to marry in August 2011; and then something went wrong. It was called off and we each found new partners. Mine was somebody, met at a dinner for singles given by an old friend from Oxford days (Baroness Greenfield, no less, was there). I will call her Jonquil Haitch.* She had been an actress, indeed she had been a Bond girl; and she was doing a Ph.D. in something called *qualitative psychology* at one of the London colleges under the supervision of a certain Professor Kentigern Jones.* I could not make much sense of qualitative psychology at the dinner though initially I felt sympathetic to the way it seemed to be putting philosophy to work. As our short relationship continued the grim truth emerged. You see, the kind of psychology that I do — you know, the dreary bean-counting stuff — is *quantitative* psychology that fails to get to the heart of the holistic lived experience, the nub of human mental life.

Jonquil's research for her Ph.D. involved giving semi-structured interviews to ten men (only ten; let's not be *quantitative*) on what it was like to be retired. One of the men lived in Aberdeen. What happened to these interviews? Kentigern's group did not go in for discourse analysis of the kind done by Peregrine Trotter (p.120 above). Rather what people said was illuminated by reference — don't ask me how — to the phenomenological philosophers such as Husserl and Sartre; indeed Heidegger got a look-in too ("We're all Heideggerians!" enthused Jonquil one day).

A word about phenomenology, the philosophical school that makes experience its centrepiece. One could say that it all began with the Transcendental Aesthetic section of Kant's *Critique* (see p. 224), with "aesthetic" referring to sensibility (though as ever the Greeks were probably there first). Recall the discussion above about the "a priori of space and time," these being necessary features of experience. Husserl though was more of a Cartesian insofar as he treated sensibility as a kind of bedrock. He spoke of "bracketing" (*Einklammerung*) — or *epoché*, a Greek term for a Greek notion — of all our assumptions about the external world in order to confront experience/sensibility in the raw. That's all I'll say. I have never particularly bothered with phenomenology (since my Birkbeck days at least); though some philosophers of mind whom I deeply respect take it seriously. Well, it is obvious even from these few words that phenomenology is all about the *first person*. It is about how, through this first-person bracketing, one can confront a kind of epistemic bottom-line. Given this, you cannot, *in this strict sense*, talk about the phenomenology of another person. How could this mental content be expressed through the medium of language? My phenomenology is not something I can share we you. Not because it is "private" (Wittgenstein did not die in vain), but because to ask for my phenomenology is simply to betray your lack of understanding of what Husserl and others were talking about.

At this point I tack back briefly to the personal. Carole and I had kept in touch (in fact, we — well I did anyway — regarded our schism as a time-out, rather than a final break. We married in December 2013). She gave me as a Christmas present: Mark Ford's wonderful translation of Raymond Roussel's — he was a sort of proto-surrealist, unique really — poem *Nouvelles Impressions d'Afrique.* I devoured it, enjoying especially his obsessive bracketing, and the remorseless dredging of each figurative move in the poem — a hilarious kind of thoroughness. Then, on our last day together Jonquil said to me: "Why can't we have a *properly nuanced* discussion for once" (this was clearly a phrase much in use among these Heideggerian psychologists).

I went away and wrote a long satirical poem, a single sentence, in Roussel's bracketing mode (a row of 120 closed brackets on the final page) — *Properly Nuanced: Raymond Roussel's Form Falls upon the New Psychology.*[88] It was supposed to read like the translation of a poem and was a very far cry from Wallace Stevens. This was how I introduced the research programme:

> — *the subjective actuality; the holistic quiddity; the what-*
> *it-is-likeness; the how-it-is-with-me-ness; the perspectival*
> *and experiential point; the self's projection (if not the soul's*
> *locus); the innerly not-a-something-but-not-a-nothing either*
> *(as that tiresomely un-phenomenological thinker Wittgenstein*
> *put it); the unique epistemic stance; the pad from which*
> *the propositional attitudes are launched; the source of*
> *and the convergence point of all true (i.e., qualitative)*
> *mental states; in short, the stuff of the NEW PSYCHOLOGY)));*
> *and, given all this, does Kenny point his students*

---

[88] Knives, Forks, and Spoons Press, 2012

towards the calculator, the logarithms, the number-crunching
software and the tables of statistical significance ("of
insignificance" quips Kentigern).....the voice trails
off and a smile plays upon the lips, for you feel
the enormous No stirring like a something in the
Lederhosen of a well-lunched burgher; — like
a rumble above the mountains when the sky darkens;
— like petite perceptions of a hundred hooves
of cattle growing impatient; — like the thrum below decks
when the ferry sways and stirs itself; — like
an incipient throat-clear of an actor of
the Kenneth Granham kind (maybe playing a
paterfamilias in Pinter); — the raspy hum of a
stutterer as he (it is usually a 'he' isn't it?) approaches
weak-kneed a word hurdle; —the PA system
of a rock band when the band is between numbers
and trying to intimidate the audience; — the groaning
of a redwood before it topples somewhere in California))
until the mighty affirmation ascends from Norbeck audible
to the very gates of University College and east to good
Queen Mary; for No! — he tells them to open their Heidegger;
for is he not the founder of P.H.A.R.T. — Phenomenological,
Hermeneutical Analytical Research Trajectory — (pausing to note
that Kenny insists upon 'trajectory': it is an ongoing, dynamic,
upwardly-thrusting process (no stasis wanted on board) as this
is no limp Scientia that "bids the passing moment stay" (any more
than a micturator or evacuator could stem the process once
in train; — any more than a tired-of-life-and-challenged-by-it
could back-pedal upwards from the ledge of Beachy Head
(though note the clear dis-analogy here, as the P.H.A.R.T.
trajectory is ever upwards); –

Jonquil had described her initial interview with Kentigern at which he had given her a passage of Heidegger to construe ...

> *when (at their first meeting with Professor*
> *Kentigern Jones) Kenny gives them a passage of Heidegger*
> *of eye-watering obscurity ("It is as if," a sceptical colleague said,*
> *"they are invited to yank fishhooks into their poor old cheeks")*
> *and tells them to go home and "write down just what this means to*
> *you in yourself"; while, on reading the hilarities, he says "You were*
> *challenged Miss [Tuber] and you have risen to the challenge.*
> *I see great potential to be tapped by the bradawl of application.*
> *Now off you pop to Planet Organic, sweetness, and bring me*
> *a coffee."))))) and which is the pith and kernel of P.H.A.R.T, whose*
> *empirical contents are vertiginous but grounded, whose methodology*
> *is Simple-Simon but whose epistemic contexts are superfine and*
> *ink-wrought: one simply asks the participants (as few as possible*
> *(as quantity is the enemy of a hermeneutic enterprise))"what is it*
> *like to do X?" (e.g., what is it like to be unemployed, with no*
> *money and many dependents (really, how is it for you, innerly?);*

I had huge fun writing the piece, but it was fuelled by anger, which sometimes comes over as simple nastiness in the text. But how did Kentigern get to this position? He is doing wonderfully well: a professorship in one of the best psychology departments in the UK, grant money galore. Grant money! Yes. The NHS seems to like the idea of this sterile journalism as a way of finding out how their patients are getting on "innerly." I am vague about Kentigern's CV. I believe that after a first degree in an arts subject he did a conversion course in psychology after which a Ph.D. with — no surprises here — Rom Harré at Oxford (p.122 above). I have never met him. To get on as he does he must have messianic self-belief.

Why not just let this go? Why all the anger? Not just because P.H.A.R.T.* (recall: Phenomenological, Hermeneutical Analytical Research Trajectory) is proof of what happens when we abandon the idea that psychology is an experimental science designed to uncover the mechanisms that enable us to do what we can do. Not just because it's an egregious example of psychology of the ghostly, what-makes-us tick school, that brings a kind of shamanistic specialist knowledge — how's your Heidegger? — to the task of reporting on what people are like/how it is with them. Because it's so successful: it's actually *thriving*. It's a real-and-present danger. Before she moved to King's London my daughter Charlotte had a lectureship in a psychology department in which practitioners of P.H.A.R.T. (often ex-nurses) were appointed to posts over cognitive neuroscientists, in which the weaker students were being kept happy on a diet of this pretentious pabulum. In the next section we shall see how the qualitative tide is lapping Cambridge.

I also find it difficult to laugh off the fact that well-heeled people like Jonquil who can afford the fees (she practices as a "existential" psycho-therapist too), can actually gain a Ph.D. from this baloney. I contrast her with my current graduate student — brilliant, working class, state-funded. He has to struggle with the fact that two experiments that should have been the centrepiece of this thesis did not come off. With P.H.A.R.T. though you can never fail — nor succeed either.

Some psychologists reading this will just shrug and say that it's no more than the natural contempt that people in the "harder" areas of psychology feel for those doing the "softer" stuff. Not so, for the good reason that there is no continuity between experimental psychology and qualitative psychology (with P.H.A.R.T. an egregious example of it). It is true to say, though, that one does come across this kind of contempt; indeed with oneself as the victim. Most recently, I happened to meet an Italian neuroscientist from the Institute of Cognitive Neuroscience (ICN) in a pub at The Angel Islington. He was well on the way to being drunk: "Oh so you only do beHAYvioural worka. BeHAYvioural worka! You have yourra data! You have yourra *CHI-squarea!*"[89] Then a snigger. I pointed out that his colleagues at the ICN, who do neuro-imaging of theory of mind, would have nothing to do were it not for the behavioural work, chi-squares, and the *theorising* of Wimmer and Perner (p.149).

And talking of neuroscience, I should say that I'm an even-handed micky-taker. My other chapbook was called *Neurotrash*. This was not, of course, an attack on neuroscience (which would be like attacking chemistry). I do not ally myself with Ray Tallis (p.129) and his generalised attacks on neuroscienctific over-reaching. Neurotrash is the the bone-headed cartoon of neuroscience (think Paul McKenna on "neurolinguistic programming" as an extreme case). It is usually written by "writers" who have to write about something, by journalists, and even occasionally by

---

[89] A simple statistical test

neuroscientists who've been sweet-talked by publishers. Some people make a jolly good living from it, people who know nothing about the brain, yet can string together sentences with the following format: "Studies show...the hypothalamus... a structure called the amygdala... Apparently..." Jonathan Miller once identified something called the "apparently syndrome;" and there is a lot of that in neurotrash. "It turns out that ..." is a handy phrase too .A popular bit of neurotrash is that the (interesting but unsurprising) experiments by Benjamin Libet have shown us that free will does not exist.

Anyway, in the chapbook I was doing no more than poking gentle fun. For example, a poem called "Implicit and Explicit Processing: the Neuroscience of Wilkie Collins" was only about a girl in a New York Bar, plus some reference to *The Moonstone*.

Neurotrash aside, it is a huge mistake to think that psychology done with neuro-imaging data is *necessarily* "harder" that behavioural studies. Think of the work — done at the ICN I think — on whether the brains of left-wingers are different to those of right-wingers, inspired by an item on the *Today* programme. And, turning back to poetry, I don't know what to say about the case of a friend of mine, an ex-Cambridge undergraduate and prizewinning poet, who has just gained a doctorate on the neuroscience of poetry. Or rather, I do know what to say about it but won't; before this becomes even more like a blog.

Injury time

In 2006 I was lucky enough to become a Fellow of Queens' college. I say lucky, because academics in their late '50s who have already resigned from two colleges, and who are sub-stellar, typically struggle to find a college. I was lucky too because Queens' is a lovely college. The Fellowship came, as nearly all Fellowships do, with a teaching contract to give at least six hours of supervisions (tutorials) a week. As I could not fulfil this contract by developmental psychology teaching alone I was supervising on everything from hearing to human evolution. It was this experience that forced me to think about the nature of psychology and where it's heading; and gave rise to this book. What's more, I became Director of Studies (DoS) in the Psychological and Behavioural Sciences Tripos (PBST). And, at this the tone darkens; as if it weren't dark enough already.

I need to explain the background to PBST. As I mentioned at the very start of the Cambridge section (with reference to the late Cathy Urwin of the Childcare and Development Group) psychology of a social and developmental kind was also done in the Social Sciences Faculty. In fact, developmental psychology carried on in parallel within the university: people like me in Experimental Psychology and Martin Richards over in the Faculty of Social and Political Studies (SPS) in Free School Lane. There was a basic split between psychology as a biological science and as a social science. Stranger still was the fact that Cambridge was the only university in the UK to which it was impossible to apply to study psychology. School pupils could apply to read social science and specialise in psychology of a social kind, and they could apply to read natural science or medicine and specialise in experimental psychology; and that was it. Due to the tireless efforts of my colleague Mike Aitken and the determined negotiating of our head of department Trevor Robbins the two departments merged and offered the PBST as a degree in psychology in 2012. This was something that eventually had to happen. I am glad it did happen; though the rest of this section will not give that impression.

At Queens' I used to supervise students from what had become the Department of Social and Developmental Psychology (then within the "Faculty of Politics, Psychology, Sociology and International Studies," if you must know). Indeed, because social psychology was taught within our second-year Experimental Psychology option I found myself teaching social psychology to committed social psychologists; indeed found myself revealing to them my deep distrust of most social psychology. One feisty young woman fought back. To my charge that there was nothing you could call a serious theory in social psychology, she gave me Serge Moscovici's *social representations theory*; and to my charge that the social-experimental outcomes were either banal or un-replicable or both, she gave me the Moscovici's work on *minority influence*.

Let's take these two in turn. I had first heard about Moscovici from the lips of (now "the late") Gerard Duveen from the social faculty. It seemed pretty interesting stuff; and certainly Moscovici had led an interesting life. A Jew born in Romania in 1925, he left his home country and settled in Paris a couple of years after the war, becoming friendly with his fellow Romanian Jew Paul Celan, the great modernist poet of the holocaust. Perhaps through his experiences of fascism, Zionism and communism he became interested in the way our beliefs are constructed through regnant social structures and modes of communication. Indeed, in how the transfer of information within groups affects the content of what is transferred — *a la* Chinese whispers. In particular, he studied the way in which the reception of psychoanalysis within France depended upon the social milieu into which it was introduced — Catholic, communist, liberal, and so forth.

As time went on this developed into something that became known as social representations theory, which is the general view that what we think about something is a function of the way we represent how others within our social group think about it. How much of this is simple compliance? Not much, Moscovici argued, because if it were then we would all think alike; which we do not. He argued instead for minority influence: the process whereby the still small voices of members of a minority can influence the majority view. If, by contrast, it is the majority influencing the minority then all we have is compliance. In the first place there is genuine representational change, and in the second mere giving in with no real mental change at all – just behavioural change.

Turning to the evidence for this we find the reason for my feisty student's defence of social psychological experiments. There is a huge amount of work on compliance within social psychology (of an individual to the majority) and it is just as boringly tautological as I said it was. There is, however, evidence (originally from Moscovici and Personnaz, 1980[90]) that not only *is* there a minority effect, but that it causes real representational change — even in how you represent a colour. Imagine you are in a group looking at a purpley-blue colour patch. While most of you say it's blue, one person insists it is red, causing you to introspect hard on your colour experience until you find you are literally seeing red. How do the experimenters know you really see red and are not just agreeing with the pest to get out and on with your life? Because you report that when you look at a white sheet of paper straight afterwards you see a green *afterimage*. Those who stick to the blue answer report seeing a yellow afterimage. Intriguing certainly, not least for what it implies about the "cognitive penetrability[91]" of colour qualia — quite apart from the social aspects.

What to say to all this? As regards social representations theory, it is not a theory at all. Perhaps the acid test for whether a theory has content is whether its negation makes sense. Well, it's clear nonsense to say that the way we think about subjects is *unaffected* by the way we represent others' views about them. Also, who would deny that things like madness, gender, and old age are represented within different social groups in different ways? As *psychology*, it is vacuous. Within sociology, however, that kind of interest — call it that rather than "theory"

---

[90]   Moscovici, S., & Personnaz, B. (1980). Studies in social influence: Minority influence and conversion behaviour in a perceptual task. *Journal of Experimental Social Psychology, 16,* 270–282.

[91]   Meaning how perception is influenced by belief – much discussed in the literature on mental imagery.

— can be a starting point for empirical investigation into such matters as religious belief (e.g., as in Durkheim's "collective representations"), political views, cultural identity, and so forth. But if you think that by saying things like "social representation is the level at which the individual relates to society, linking objects, subjects and activities" you have a handle on anything other than thin air you're wrong. It does, though, give you a kind of never-can-lose fecundity, where links can be made to anything that takes your fancy — discourse analysis, and all the stuff I talked about under Peregrine Trotter. With regard to king-of-the-ghosts psychology, the case is very simple: the psychologist has the illusion that social representations theory is telling him or her something about what people are like. They are highly social in their way of thinking (well blow me down!).

What about the empirical cash-value of Moscovici's views — minority influence? I was certainly impressed by the after-image work and would tell supervisees about it; though I did not bother to chase down further papers on the topic (I have never really overcome a better-things-to-do attitude, so much in evidence in my days as post-grad demonstrator at Birkbeck). However, in 2011 I went to Gröningen to give a talk and met a lively group of social psychologists. The after-image result, they told me, has turned out to be an artefact,[92] and the minority influence effect has to be so hedged around with

---

[92] See Martin, R (1998) Majority and minority influence using the afterimage paradigm: A series of attempted replications. *Journal of Experimental Social Psychology, 34,* 1–26 (1998)

qualifications that it has small predictive or explanatory value.[93]

Now back to the social-experimental merger. It was inevitable that once the merger took place the experimental psychologists would have the whip hand. None-the-less, the PBST psychology course was and remains heavily social. There was plenty of developmental psychology in it, but often of a social kind (e.g., peer relations).

Shortly before the merger with the Department of Social and Developmental Psychology I looked at the web-pages of some of the people who were to become my new colleagues. Reporting on two of them will be more than enough. "Read with mounting horror" is the cliché. In fact I began with horror and ended with whimpering despair. First was Dr. Hermione Hayre-Ball.* She has used social representations theory in her work and is interested in "the genesis, transformation, and interaction between representations." She uses qualitative as well as quantitative methods, is interested in focus groups and narrative interviews and also "in assessing the quality of qualitative work" (why not be interested in representations of the quality of the quality of qualitative work?). A glance at the list of publications shows a further interest in representations of mental health..."clients' representations of mental health problems" and the like. For all I know, some of this stuff may be quite interesting, but from my perspective, the difference between an interest in mental health and an interest in representations of mental health is not unlike the difference

[93] See R. Martin and M. Newston (2003) Majority versus minority influence: When, not whether, source status instigates heuristic or systematic processing. *European Journal of Social Psychol. 33*, 313–330

between sex and pornography.

In passing, just a few months ago I read an ethics-committee application from Hayre-Ball's group. The study they wanted to do involved visiting hairdressers specialising in Afro-Caribbean hair and interviewing, in the sterile-journalistic way of qualitative psychology, women who were returning from "relaxed" (straightened) hair to *au naturel* hair. These interviews would be interpreted in terms of Moscovici's social representations theory.

Things could only get better. They didn't. Next up was Fabian Klein, hardly thought about since 1969. Here was his now-beardless face, like a face whose owner had just been told: "Give your best shot at miming twinkly-smug satisfaction or we will kill you." His big idea now was "Personal Life-Optimisation by Projects"* (or P.L.O.P.* theory). There were links to his recent YouTubed talks, to his interviews, and to noodle testimonials (this I did *not* make up): "In his presentations – which are both deeply informative and outrageously funny – [Professor Klein] helps his audiences learn how to make effective use of these personality differences. *'A cross between Robin Williams and Einstein'* is how one client described him" (emphasis added). How did he find his way through the highly permeable membrane of Free School Lane psychology? As a "distinguished scholar." It is the "scholar" bit that takes the biscuit.

Watching as much of Klein's performances as I could bear — there is a TED talk now — I was reminded of Pascal once again: "All men's miseries derive from not being able to sit in a quiet room alone." The modern version might be: "All men's miseries derive from not being able to sit down and keep quiet." As the waves of snake-oil verbiage rolled on, it became clear that here was a rabbit that thought it was King of the Ghosts.

I only had a handful of years to go before I retired, so my instinct was to keep my head down and let them get on with it. Let it go. This option was not open to me, however, as I'd agreed, as I said, to be the Director of Studies (DoS) in PBST at Queens.' This meant I was obliged to interview applicants, generally keep an eye on their progress, and maybe give them some supervisions too.

As the large majority of the applicants had taken A-Level Psychology, and as part of the assessment process involved their sending in two essays for me and the other interviewer to read, I read an awful lot of A-level psychology essays. Covered in ticks they were, with one tick meaning a point. I came to regard much of A-Level Psychology as something that was not so much education as a kind of drill. I mean like drill in the army, the kind that's done merely to keep the soldiers occupied— painting the coal white, for example. The kind that soldiers call "bullshit." Why paint the coal white? It gets you dirty and burning paint makes dangerous fumes. Why set questions on Stanley Milgram's obedience "experiments?" They teach you no more that a nasty bit of social history, and the experiments were exercises in sadism. Yes indeed, but the quality of coal-painting and of Milgram-nouse can be assessed; and any fool can supervise either of them. That's the beauty of it.

Needless to say, there was the Milgram experiment in the PBST course, so let me now say just why I find this stuff so difficult to admire. Milgram had a sort of sociological project which was to raise the possibility, post WW2, that Americans were, no less than the Germans and those they occupied, hardly averse to "just following orders" (Eichman's phrase). The participants in the experiments were duped all down the line, before, during, and long after the study. As far as they were concerned they were taking part in an experiment on human learning in which they had to teach somebody in the next room how to do a task by administering electric shocks as negative feedback. This "learner" was in fact a stooge — a confederate of the experimenter. Initially the shocks were mild, then, as the stooge failed to improve, the participants were encouraged to increase the voltage. The shock levels on the machine were labelled from "SLIGHT SHOCK" to "DANGER—SEVERE SHOCK" and finally "XXX." Yes, indeed, a large number of the unfortunates who had volunteered for the study ended up giving the stooge mammoth doses of electricity — XXX — despite his pleading and convulsive twitching. That's it. The white-coated experimenters would intone: "The experiment must continue;" and it did.

I could add that Zimbardo's "prison" experiment,[94] which also featured in these essays, exists within the same grisly domain.

---

[94] In Zimbardo's Stanford Prison Experiment students were randomly assigned to the roles of "prisoner" or "guard." The latter were given to psychological torture of the former.

Needless to say, this was a study of *what people are like* — it was ghost psychology: people are potentially passive fascists (ironic that the bullying of the participants was done in the name of science). An intelligent twelve-year-old knows the study itself was not science. People are pretty various and some are indeed easy to bully. Some, too, are cruel. Some, indeed, are mentally unstable, and psychologically torturing them is not conducive to their wellbeing.

For me, this saga tells us far less about the participants than it does about the experimenters. Who would want to put on a white coat and stand over some poor sweating creature (almost certainly somebody poorer and less educated than you) as he twisted the dial a further notch at your insistence? Who would want to send him away thinking he had nearly killed somebody because he was so weak-minded? Who was just following orders — the orders of Professor Milgram who was supervising your work and maybe writing letters of reference for you? Who were the fascists here? The boss whose orders had to be followed was merely an ambitious academic.

This is almost more to the point, I think, than the fact that the conduct of the study was dishonest to an immoral degree, as has been chronicled in Gina Perry's excellent book *Behind the Shock Machine*[95] (some participants were not debriefed until long after the study was finished, and others were *never* debriefed). Now, let me unglue my hands from this tar-baby and get back to the PBST applicants.

---

[95] The experimenters were supposed to stop telling the participants to continue after four iterations. But this was not the case: often they continued insisting the study must continue long after four.

Otherwise, the essays were mainly on security of attachment of toddler to mother, depression, sex differences, and the "social learning" of aggression. This last was nearly as coal-paintingly pointless as the Milgram work. If you show children an adult punching a Bobo doll (which are designed to be punched) they will, uh, punch it. So this shows of course that aggression is like *learned*. Tick, tick.

The applicants were a mixed bag, who only had in common their complete ignorance of the cognitive level of explanation. If they had any views at all about psychology, they equated it with social psychology. We did offer a place to a bright spark who had not taken A-Level psychology, while later taking a young lady sight-unseen through the pool. I'll call them The Bright Spark and The Young Lady.

I decided to supervise these two and some other people from Queens' who were taking the PBST introductory course as an option. These supervisions did not go well. For one thing, I was damned if I was going to discuss "psycho-geography" (no, not Situationism, nor Ian Sinclair, nor Will Self! I mean *geographical psychology*) with anybody. Or indeed the Big Five personality traits theory that it's based on— the O.C.E.A.N. (outgoingness, consciousness, extraversion, agreeableness, neuroticism) traits. As a friend at Queens' said, it's like The Beach Boys: "The East coast girls are conscientious, I really dig those styles they wear, but the Southern girls with their neurotic streaks they knock me out when I'm down there."

The crash came one Monday afternoon as I started to read a student essay on "close relationships," a topic taught by Igor

Facebook,* a bouncing social psychologist of well-being (F. Klein is very big on this too) who is also interested in the love hormone (oxytocin: "It smells like turpentine, it tastes of Indian Ink."[96] Did you know that people high on the neuroticism part of O.C.E.A.N. have shorter marriages? Did you know that people high on conscientiousness make better employees?) It was an essay by The Bright Spark. Actually it began well, but I simply could not read past the first page. It was the topic – not him. I immediately emailed my Queens' supervisees, cancelled the supervision, told them to stop writing their essays, and to write one instead on face perception (based on lectures by an experimental-psychologist colleague). The Bright Spark protested to me by email. Instead of doing this, others went straight to the Senior Tutor to complain about my teaching. Now, I have been guilty of some bad teaching in my time, some comically bad teaching, but nobody has ever actually *complained*. (As I write this some Frank O'Hara lines come to mind:

> *I have been to lots of parties*
> *and acted perfectly disgraceful*
> *but I never actually collapsed.*[97]

I agreed with the Senior Tutor that I should stop supervising PBST. My reaction was one of relief, with an undercurrent of Teddy-Smaile-like truculence ... "No skin off my nose guv," I said to myself in my Language of Thought.

---

[96] *Love Potion Number Nine* by the Coasters

[97] His poem that begins "Lana Turner has collapsed"

There was a further step down. In the subsequent vac I received a "Dear Jim" email from the PBSTers. They asked me to arrange for them some supervisions on statistics with a certain Dr. X about whom they had heard good reports. I sent two emails, one asking them not to address me as "Jim" — I said I should have "nipped this in the bud"— and one pointing out that supervision-arranging is not at all like "middle class parents" fixing up extra tuition to boost their child's performance. This time the "middle-class parents" themselves were up-in-arms and the Senior Tutor suggested that I give up being the DoS. I refused. But later, all was more-or-less repaired (I am a great believer in apologising). The excellent James Kelly (the Senior Tutor) and I went back to being on friendly terms, and some time later I was delighted to receive a box of chocolates and a nice note from The Bright Spark thanking me for my help and wishing me a happy retirement.

Yes, of course, this little saga reveals my class sensitivity (a class warrior in a matchstick universe) and my petulance, indeed the unprofessionalism I'm capable of. Self-flagellation is not the point here. The point is that one can be brought face-to-face with the fact that psychology had not moved on. Far from coming of age it is still lying in bed till noon calling down to its mum for a bacon butty.

I did acquire self-control, of sorts, about all this (I learned to use my pre-frontal lobes rather than my amygdala, as the neurotrashers would put it). The Young Lady told me much later that she was particularly excited by Dr. Hayre-Ball's lectures on qualitative methods and Moscovici. I tried to organise my sphinx-like face.

I realised that through being embedded in Cambridge psychology for the past 28 years I'd been living in a bubble — a professional one, unlike the personal one of my Birkbeck days. Outside the bubble (the bubble membrane ending just across the road from Pembroke college where Free School Lane begins) were just the kind of creatures I thought had retired to their woodwork homes long ago. I was the victim of an *esse-est-percipii* delusion: if I did not see them then they weren't there. Psychology as cognitive science (a collaboration between experimental psychology, computer modelling, and philosophy) and as cognitive neuroscience (studying cognition, perception, learning and emotion by reference to what we know about brain function from imagining, invasive work with laboratory animals, and work with patients) were beginning to feel like elements of a minority interest.

The nadir was a staff meeting held over in the Free School Lane site. White gloss on brick, high windows, metal fixtures: the meetings room was like an enormous prison cell. Fabian Klein was on my right, Hermione Hayre-Ball on my left, and in front of me one of my new colleagues was discoursing. She finds, by the way, that people who prove, from a questionnaire, to have a low sense of personal power tend to see objects as farther away from them than the high-personal-power merchants. Or is it vice versa? I'll get back to you on that. The only positive aspect was that I could hardly hear what was going on due to the terrible acoustics and the fact that I'd killed off so many of my auditory hair cells by bombarding my head-phoned ears with loud music (Stones, Wagner, Slayer) in the drinking years. Anyway, "hair cells" is only a social construct, if you get my drift. I should re-interrogate my notion of "good hearing."

On that bit of snidery I should re-insist that my target has not simply been social psychology. As there is neurotrash, there is cognotrash, written by experimental psychologists who really should know better. There is the kind of psychology — usually in "popular" books; but undergraduates read them — that advertise deep truths about The Mind woven into a pattern from experimental studies. Take the case of Steve Cowl.* Steve is a good experimental psychologist, indeed a careful and creative one; and he also does the kind of outreach work that most academic psychologists would never think of doing. But when Steve has what he takes to be a big and good idea he doesn't write a piece to send out to academic journals that publish theory papers. He instead writes books with simple take-home messages smuggled out under the academic wire for a general audience. So what? Not only can these be icing without a cake, but their popular reception can persuade the author that he is really on to something — air for the ego.

I never gave Steve much thought until one day when I was looking at a display of psychology books in Heffers' window, and there was *Reasons Why "You" Don't Actually Exist** by Steven Cowl. He argues that the idea of there being a "me" — a self — is merely an illusion that the brain constructs for us:[98] not a *concept* — an *illusion*. Hang on. In what sense is it an

---

[98]   There is a huge philosophical literature, much of it Kantian, on the unity of consciousness. Obviously the brain must support this core element of selfhood … a mere "construct?"

illusion? If that is an illusion, what's the reality? We do indeed have a sense of self and we would not have this unless the brain processed information in a certain way. But reviewing what the

brain does — actually it is a kitchen sink book, even Zimbardo gets a look-in — is not to reveal the tricks of an illusion-monger.

By the way, it's important not to confuse that patently silly claim with the philosophical position that our everyday notion of "the self" is incoherent: that the way we put the notion of "self" to use in our thinking is inherently contradictory or empty. That was David Hume's view and it is Derek Parfit's view.[99] For Parfit, this incoherence extends to the idea of self-interest and thus into the moral realm, not to mention the religious (Buddhist) realm. These views should not be confused with Steve's shiny-faced gung ho.

On the cover of the book Brand Smarmer[*] (a neuroscience *writer* of course), author of *Your Brain, your Friend,*[*] says: "Steve Cowl is one of the most profound thinkers of our age" (the verb-phrase is *not* made up). Cowl is no dunce. So, why does he join this confederacy of dunces? The wrong kind of ambition of course.

This is not about illustrating the folly of one man. It is to show a commonality between this kind of thing and the ghostliness of Kentigern Jones' P.H.A.R.T. (as an extreme case). In both cases — Jones with his Heidegger and Cowl with his shocking revelation about the self not existing — we

---

[99] See: Derek Parfit, *Reasons and Persons* (Oxford: Oxford University Press, 1984).

have faux, if not fraudulent, profundity targeted at the naïve. And we have inflation of the ego.

"Self's the man," otherwise. Shortly after writing the above paragraph a publisher's notice came onto my phone saying the following about a new book from this once serious publisher:[100] "This book provides an analysis of the social representations of leading self-help genres, including neurolinguistic programming, cognitive self-help therapy, mindfulness, self-management, self-esteem, self-leadership and self-control. Exploring the globalised therapeutic culture of today, the book argues that psychology as 'science' is often abandoned to aid the individual pursuit for self-realization and self-optimization." It's like Christmas morning, with all the favourites there — not only social representations but neurolinguistic programming. Nice touch with the scare quotes round the word science too.

Well, I did give this last section the heading "injury time." The reader must be exhausted by this stream of beleaguered negativity. And the final whistle blows a sad note. In February 2015 Nick Mackintosh died at the age of 79 after a short illness. He was the first academic psychologist I met. I can't say he was a mentor. He was more important than that. He was somebody I would think of during my all-to-frequent dark nights of the professional soul. Psychology must be worth a darn, if Nick's a psychologist.

---

[100] Readers who enjoyed *Psychology as King of the Ghosts* by James Russell will certainly not enjoy *Optimising the Self: Social Representations of Self-Help* by Ole Jacob Madsen, published by the house which published Piaget's books in English.

Reflections

Jerry Bruner called his autobiography *In Search of Mind*. He didn't find it (it certainly did not exist in a law faculty). Well, I did not find it either; and I hope my failure is exemplary. I began with the idea that there is something called The Mind. It has a certain character, hidden from us, and individual minds are mere exemplars of it. We study the mind by constructing big theories of what people are like. That's what psychology is. Rather late in my career (supervising social psychology at Queens') I came to the view that this project is doomed to fail, and that psychology is the study of how we can do what we can do – the underlying mechanisms. Outside of this is ego-inflation, pseudo-science, and dullness — a ghost territory.

I have not *demonstrated* this of course. I have been showing, rather than telling, saying: "Look how things turned out for me." These are the blind alleys, the wading through bullshit, the grandiosity of ambition, the fantastical immodesty encountered and sometimes evinced. In doing this showing there has been chattiness and ad hominem aggression; but I have not been settling scores. I do *indeed* think a lot of the people I encountered or heard about in my career are frauds, frauds who've been lucky to make a living from psychology. Some of the material about myself was there just to make the point that actually I am not somebody with a superhumanly incisive intellect who can see straight to the heart of this folly. I simply learn from experience. And some of the personal material is there to show that a lot depends on *who* is doing which kind of psychology. The distinction between king-of – the-ghosts psychology and the type I advocate is not a formal one, depending as it does on who is doing it and how.

Now is the time to give an impersonal-as-I-can-manage defence of the positions that I have been simply asserting.

Part Three:

Questioner. *You say that ghost psychology wrongheadedly studies The Mind: "For I shall be arguing that the notion of The Mind as an object of study is an incoherent notion, because there are only minds, and minds are points-of-view — individuals' views from somewheres. There cannot be a view from everywhere." This requires a proper defence. We talk about "the brain," so why not "the mind"?*

JR. It's important to distinguish between capacities and dispositions. What I am saying is that the mind considered as a set of dispositions is an incoherent idea. I think of a disposition as a point on a scale. For example, we have the capacity to respond to events with emotions of various kinds, and people vary in terms of how emotionally reactive they are. To make this clearer I will refer to $mind_d$ (dispositional mind) and $mind_c$ (capacity mind). Only the latter makes sense, on my view. In terms of $mind_c$ we have the mind as an entity that can see, hear, think, speak and so forth. As regards $mind_d$, however, we have an entity with the average of all human dispositions: extrovert, introvert too, averagely disposed to jealousy, both given to cognitive dissonance and not, not particularly fearful nor bold either. The only thing we can say about such an entity is that nothing can be said about the content of its dispositions at all; and this is something *defined* in terms of dispositions. So, we have described a non-entity. Its only essential character is as something with capacities, with a potential to, say, show emotion and so forth. It has no essential character though.

Q. *But how can you equate a particular point-of-view with a particular set of dispositions?*

JR. I equate them insofar as they both stand out as being distinct from the bad idea of a generalised set of dispositions ($mind_d$) and generalised set of points-of-view (both literally spatial and "how things seem to me now"). Think of the latter in terms of consciousness. While there can be particular conscious states, the idea of just "conscious states in general" makes no sense. What could be the content, the aboutness,[101] of such a generalised consciousness? All actual and possible worlds? What does make sense though is a generalised capacity to have such states — what psychology ought to study, I think.

Q. *But you have made no clear link between an exclusive interest in $mind_d$ and what you call king-of-the-ghosts psychology.*

JR. I am thinking of the possibility of a body of knowledge of what people are like. Psychologists who see themselves as contributing to this body of knowledge — doing experiments on obedience, attribution, aggression,

---

[101] Franz Brentano claimed that thought has Intentionality or aboutness. Mental acts take an object that will have, in his terminology "intentional inexistence." More informally, one cannot simple be conscious: there must be an object of the comscious state.

affiliation, and so forth — are clearly interested in what people are disposed to do, rather than explaining how they do what they can do (e.g., reading, seeing, reasoning, showing emotion).

Q. *And what's wrong with that!*

JR. What's wrong with it is that it is ultimately nothing more than reportage. If I am right about the non-existence of $mind_d$ then it is impossible for these data about the conditions under which people are aggressive and all the rest of it to be knowledge of something. At the very least, it is not knowledge in the sense in which we have knowledge, say, about how we process visual information or develop mentally. This distinction can also be seen in a statistical light. Think of the kind of data you end up with in studies of $mind_d$ versus $mind_c$. I know there is a lot of debate these days about Frequentist versus Bayesian models in statistics that may or may not be relevant to what I am about to say; but here goes: we can distinguish between two views of what statistical testing tells us. On the one hand there is a probability value that tells us about the chances of there *being something there*. For example, you see what may be a flare at sea and are uncertain if it is signal or noise and you assign a probability to its being a signal — of there being something there.   Or behaviourally, you ask whether some principle or concept is understandable by 5 year-old children. Is this capacity there? But *alternatively*, you set up a number of situations and find that, more often than not, people in group A are more compliant than people in group B. There is no sense in which there is anything *there* in the latter case. It is more similar to "eight out of ten cats prefer *Whiskas*." You could say that a disposition to compliance is stronger in one group, and in saying this you are saying nothing more than that they comply more. Compare Molière's famous line in *Le Malade Imaginaire*: someone explains how opium puts people to sleep by the fact that it has a 'dormitive virtue'.

Q.   *But to call all this king-of-the-ghost psychology is a bit florid isn't it?*

JR.   I was coming to that. On the basis of the experiments you have run you find various trends. For example, you may find that group A people are more impulsive and that they are more likely to twiddle with any object you put in front of them — that's the statistical trend.   Then you develop a theory explaining compliance as a function of impulse control. Call it the "impulsivity nexus" theory of compliance.   You have created an entity with no ontological referent. It is not a theory of "how the mind works," or of the mind's basic character. It floats free. And then it takes on a ghostly life of its own. It gives people like Fabian Klein something to talk about, it gives therapists something to seem to be wise about; it generates examination questions. But, it is not based on anything being *there*. Of course, it may lead to research in social neuroscience — the brain correlates of excessive compliance; and that's another story.

Q. *But quite apart from the king-of the-ghosts business, are you really saying that psychologists are unable to make non-trivial generalisations about "what people are like," in the sense that how they are predisposed to behave or express emotions when certain things happen to them? Take your own example of Bowlby's work on maternal deprivation. Even those who do not take the Bowlbyan view of things will say that children have certain emotional needs and if these are not met (by loss or lack of a maternal figure or figures) then things will go wrong for them. This is premised on very reasonable assumptions about what people are like. Your attack is on an absurdly broad front.*

JR. OK, why are these assumptions about what people are like "very reasonable"? Because they are embedded in essentially mechanistic theories about *capacities*: Lorenz on imprinting and Freud on psycho-sexual development. And, even if they were based on folk-theories about our innate need for predictable nurturance much the same would follow.

What I said about Freudian theory — and I mean Freud himself, not the ever-spreading backwash — was that it is a theory about how we "keep it together." Applied to maternal deprivation, the idea is that this is how the mechanism can go wrong, giving rise to the generalisations. Staying with Freud, my gut feeling is that he was correct about the existence of the oral, anal, and phallic types of character — consequences of libidinal over-spending. These are generalisations about what people are like that grow *from a capacity theory*. Whether they arise from early rearing is a purely empirical question of course. The approaches I am arguing against are not like this. They're theories that have nothing to say about capacity at all — Moscovici just one example. They are just free-floating generalisations about this thing human nature.

Q. *I suspect you may be playing fast and loose with the distinction between capacity theories and your bête noires. You don't really give any formal characterisation of the difference.*

JR. Recall what I said at the very end: I leave it at the intuitive level because it all depends on how the theories are treated by individuals. Hence the extremely ad hominem nature of what I have been saying.

Q. *Let's take a more concrete case then. Your excessive realism about how psychological theories are grounded forces you to dismiss an awful lot of good psychology, psychology that even you would count as science. Kahneman and Tversky on our <u>dispositions</u> towards certain kinds of errors in reasoning, for example. You* *would dismiss the work of psychology's only Nobel Laureate?[102].*

JR. What their work does is to demonstrate that our reasoning faculty — a *capacity* — works imperfectly in some situations (so I am saying much the same as I just said about Freud). You may say that there is a parallel between being disposed to assume, in certainly very loaded circumstances, that the probability of "A&B" is actually higher than the probability of "A alone."[103] That is the failure of a capacity. It is nothing like the "failure" in evidence when somebody allows himself to be bullied into giving somebody huge electric shocks in the name of science. The latter is not the failure of a capacity: it is somebody at one extreme of the disposition we all have at some level —to obey. Obedience itself is a capacity, while dispositions lie on a continuum within that, as I said at the start with regard to emotionality. By the way, I do think — relatedly — that a lot of nonsense is talked about our "irrationality." Take the Wason Selection

---

[102] Actually, Kahneman's prize was for economics. His field is now known as behavioural economics.

[103] Linda is a student who is interested both in finance and in radical politics. What are the chances she'll become (a) a banker or (b) a banker with strong political interests. People often say (b) is more likely. But, two things occurring together is always less likely than one thing occurring. The question does though violate certain "conversational implicatures" of the kind described by H.P. Grice. It is fair to assume we are talking about Linda as a particular individual (imagine that (b) was "banker with one leg").

Task[104] that at least 80% of undergraduates fail. What we have here is a performance error only. To be "irrational" would be *to resist the explanation of where they went wrong* — which they never do! And, by the way, human judgement research inspires just as much egregious, ego-inflated wrongheadedness as found in the ghost-lovers. I heard Daniel Kahneman say last year that the reason we hear so much from the victims of economic austerity is that — as he showed in his work — losses loom larger than gains. Even setting aside the obvious fact that his research was on probability judgements, on taking a chance, not on experiencing the outcome of bad events, this is quite shameful.

Q. *OK, before we get overheated, let's us go back to something else you said in my initial quotation, which is roughly that there are only minds, and minds are points-of-view — views from "somewheres." This sounds rather ghostly to me, in the Rylean sense. You do not define a mind in terms of a brain but in terms of subjectivity — its perspective. Hardly the sort of position that would sit well with a stern realist like you.*

JR. Yes, as I have been talking about minds and brains I should say a little about how I see their relation. My position is a hybrid of what I call *descriptive dualism* and

---

[104] Rather than selecting the card that *could* prove a generalisation to be false, subjects select a card that can only be consistent with it. They look for evidence in favour of the rule, not for data that would show it to be false.

token identity theory (this latter quite a common position in the philosophy of mind). To a philosopher, holding both these positions would seem like squaring the circle. I'll explain them in turn. In descriptive dualism you admit that you cannot explain how conscious states and brain states are related but you also insist that conscious states *exist*. It is a way of not being a physicalist. Physicalists believe that only the physical exists; so, properly speaking, neural states exist while conscious states do not. As David Lewis put it, if God decided to recreate the world just as it is, all He would have to do would be to recreate the physical.

What does it mean for something to exist? The least you can say is that existing entities have temporal and spatial properties, indeed that they are in the crosshairs of these two. In the first place, conscious states have temporal properties: it took me a certain amount of time, for example, to decide to go to the sandwich van rather than the gym at lunchtime. What about spatial properties? Obviously, conscious states lack these, for they have them only insofar as their neural correlates have spatial properties. The spatial can, though, be thought of as being mental in a special sense. Allocentric space is clearly not mental (the ball is in the net) while egocentric space implies a point of view (the ball is on the/my left) and so implies an embodied perceiver facing in a certain direction. I know we can say that "the ball is on the left of the car," but this implies the car has a front, analogous to person's front: the car is facing a certain way (note the "face"), and this way of talking is parasitic on talk about embodied perceivers. I know too there are good arguments against this, but it's my working position. In any event, under descriptive dualism you assert that conscious mental states exist, despite their dependence on neural states. A nice position for a psychologist to hold, of course.

I appreciate that this is a very odd kind of existence. Yes, the mental depends upon the physical, and not vice versa. Yet we often speak of something existing despite a clear dependence: the painting of a horse exists, though it depends on a distribution of pigment. In fact the English word "exist" does not really fit the bill here.

To own up: all I am doing here is trying to say some words in support of the position most of us — I think all of us —hold intuitively. This is that there are mental worlds — not *the* mental world of course, where ghost psychology sets up camp —and that we each have one: our feelings and thoughts together with our self-ascriptions of them. For my money, there is a kind of absurdity in saying they are *really* brain states. Yes they *depend* upon brain states; which brings me to token identity theory.

Token identity theory has to be contrasted with *type* identity theory. Actually because "identity" implies the physicalism I want to avoid I must stress that I use the term in a deliberately loose way: one closer to "lining-up with" or "being essentially correlated with." A tokening of a mental event, a pain say, means the unique episode in which it happens; and this mental event is also a particular physical event. By contrast, mental events can be grouped into types, such as pains versus propositional thoughts (it is the same kind of distinction as the type-token relationship in linguistics: a tokening of "bread" is the occurrence of my keying in the letters now at 2.30 pm; whereas "bread" is a type of word, different from "butter"). So, what the token-identity view says is that it has to be the case that for every particular mental event there is a particular neural event — saying nothing about what type of event it has to be. I say: "Has to be the case" because to deny even this is to assert that particular mental events can be unanchored by neural events — yes ghostly indeed.

In passing, there are well-known problems with this "lining up" of token mental events and token physical ones, brought to our attention by Donald Davidson's notion of the *holism of the mental*. To explain: we can circumscribe a physical event in the brain quite precisely; and neuroscientists do this all the time. However, this cannot be done for the mental, because of the holistic nature of the mental. Holism? In thinking a thought one necessarily draws upon a multitude of further thoughts, actually or potentially. For example, in thinking "Time for tea" I pull in, or depend on, a host of further mental kinds. Even the relatively simple thought of tea pulls in drinking and leaves, not to mention liquid, and so on and so on. With regard to "time" there is linearly discrete progression, event, and then even more so-ons than tea (by the way, Fodor would strongly dispute all this. Plausibly, he says that a child can surely think about eating without taking this to be a kind of action. There's much to be said in the matter).

Type-identity theories, however, say that a given type of mental event *just is* a certain type of neural event. Pain *is* the firing of the C-fibres, in a similar sense to that in which water *is* H_2O, in a similar sense to that in which heat *is* molecular agitation. There are a number of problems with type-identity theory. In the first place, where knowing that water is H_2O tells us what this transparent liquid stuff is, it is not the case that finding out that being in pain involves the firing of the C-fibres tells us what pain really is (we learn, rather, its correlate/cause). H_2O is not the correlate/cause of being water. We already know what pain is; if it can be said that mental concepts contain within themselves the essence of mental phenomena.

Second, and more crucially, type-identity theories make it a kind of conceptual necessity that being in pain is the firing of C-fibres; but there is no necessity here. It is impossible for water not to be H_2O; for then it would be something else. It is certainly conceivable, though, for pain not to be C-fibre firing. Indeed, may not dream-pain, hysterical pain, a man's sympathetic labour pains, and hypnotically-induced pain all *not* involve C-fibre firing? It is empirical matter whether it does; and type-identity theories want it not to be an *empirical* matter. By contrast, water is H_2O by a kind of necessity: the kind identified by Saul Kripke.[105]

Now, all this may seem divorced from my polemics against king-of-the-ghosts psychology. It is not. If type-identity theory were true then think of the consequences for the distinction I made at the start between $mind_c$ and $mind_d$. This is the thought experiment. Suppose we could put together a three-dimensional working wetware model of "the human brain," which would be the central tendency of all the brains we have dissected and scanned — the typical brain. Such a brain would map on to $mind_c$, in the sense that it would be an instantiation of the neural underpinnings of our mental *capacities*. If type-identity theory were true it would also, necessarily, represent *mental life* — the central tendency of all mental lives, the common denominator of what it is like to be

---

[105] To explain at a rough approximation: the truths of logic and mathematics are necessities known *a priori* and those of biology and cricket are not necessarily true and are known *a posteriori*. Saul Kripke proposed a form of *a posteriori* necessity. That water is H_2O is this kind of necessity. Similarly, that Napoleon Bonaparte was born in Corsica is a kind of necessity. In the latter case his place of birth "rigidly" designates the particular man: it's "true in all possible worlds" that he was born there. The birth is a contingent, empirical fact but its role in designating Napoleon is not. Similarly, type identity theorists seem to regard statements like "pain is the activation of C-fibres" as *a posteriori* necessities.

each of us. It would map onto mind$_d$, because neural structures and mental life are one and the same thing under type identity theory. A mental life, I am assuming here, must involve dispositions; while a central tendency of human capacities does not.

Q. *I don't at all see what's wrong with the idea of, what you call, "common denominator of what it is like to be each of us." Thomas Nagel famously talked about what-it-is-like-to-be-a-bat (echolocation experience etc.), so what on earth is wrong with what-it-is-like-to-be a human person.*

JR. Imagining what it is like to be X only makes sense when you really don't know. When your imagination struggles and fails and you agree with Nagel, as do I, that it must be like *something*. His point is that is must be like something to be a particular bat: not that bat-experience has this suite of phenomenal characters. Analogising back to human psychology, we already know what it is like to have human mentality; so the "phenomenological psychologists" are telling us nothing. What is like to be human? What sort of academic subject is that?

Q. *I think it's time for me to bring us back to earth. You can hardly accuse the new field of social neuroscience of being king-of-the-ghosts psychology, can you? It is the study of the neural correlates of mental states of a social kind. Or are you worried they are correlating these with mind$_d$?*

JR. No, I am not worried by that, insofar as these are correlates with the capacity for feeling certain social attitudes or emotions. I am in fact a fan of Jean Decaty's work, mainly with children, on the neuroscience of empathy, altruism, moral reasoning, emotion, and other things. I don't see how anything I have said implies otherwise. And, of course, always bearing in mind my denial of type-identity physicalism, which would manifest itself as the view that altruism, say, *just is* the functioning of this circuit or another. Decaty's work tells about the neural structures underlying our socio-emotional capacities.

I have to say that, as mentioned before, the mere inclusion of imaging data or EEG data does not make a study scientific that was not already scientific in virtue of the intentions behind it and its structure. The work I mentioned earlier on imaging the brains of Tory voters versus Labour voters speaks to this, as does the social neuroscientific research that is technology-lead rather than hypothesis-lead. In the latter category I would place some work I heard of just the other day looking at the relation between mothers' and toddlers' EEG as they engage in joint attention (which they want to call "neural communication"). They do it because they can and the ambition is ghostian. The breakthrough in this area was made by Colwyn Trevarthen (a real neuroscientist by the way[106]) in his behavioural work on what he called primary and secondary (joint attention) intersubjectivity.[107] This leads the way — not an EEG machine you can wheel into a room.

Q. *I feel I am allowing you to get away with simply making <u>ex cathedra</u> judgements now. I need to press you harder. I think I see what you mean about ghost psychology seeming to be about a sort of mythical mind$_d$; though it is all pitched at too high a level of abstraction as ever. But in the central part of this book you apply the term "ghost psychology" or "king-of-the-ghosts psychology" far beyond the work of those interested in dispositions (main-stream social-personality people). You apply it promiscuously to any kind of psychology that is more theory-driven than the kind your taste runs to these days. We read "the same instinct that leads to king-of-the ghosts psychology leads us to feel we must work within Big Theories of The Mind" and "Psychology in general, and social psychology especially, leads its practitioners to believe that they have a special kind of insight into the human mind, rather as a plumber might have a special kind of insight into the water-management in your house". Essentially, all you are doing is confessing to a weakness throughout your career for grand theories,*

---

[106] Trevarthen worked with Sperry on the famous "split brain" experiments.

[107] Gratier, M. & Trevarthen, C. (2008). Musical narrative and motives for culture in mother-infant vocal interaction. *The Journal of Consciousness Studies, 15(10-11),* 122-158.

describing how you moved away from this, and then finally saying "Don't do what I did."

JR. I see what you mean. However, there *is* in fact a commonality between the disposition-merchants, the $mind_d$ folks, who tell us about what people are like essentially and indeed how they should live, from Harry Stack Sullivan to transactional analysis,[108] to the Milgram-Zimbardo fans etc. etc. and those who deliberately place themselves within the ambit of a theory, be this Laing, Bowbly, Freud, ethnomethodogy, Piaget, connectionism, even Chomskyan theory. In both cases what we see is faith in a certain "image of man," to use John Shotter's phrase. In the first case there is the focus on dispositions, and in the second the focus is on a set of a *priori* tenets; and in neither case will you be able to wake them from their dogmatic slumbers.

Q. *So all you are saying is the simply boring: Oh do let's be open-minded people. Or are you a kind of dust-bowl empiricalist now who thinks all research should be generated from reading The Journal of Experimental Psychology?*

JR. Well I am about to get even more boring and say, in the second case, it is a matter of degree. If you yawn at that

---

[108] This is the brain-child of Eric Berne. It is all about how people interact with one another. Think of "I'm OK, you're OK", "The Games People Play," both the book by Berne and the much-more-enjoyable and succinct hit song by Joe South.

point please remember that the differences between rich and poor is "only a matter of degree." Let me explain: you may need to be a subscriber to some strong theoretical position to get your work off the ground; and indeed when you critique the work of others it is usually from a contrasting theoretical position, not just because you don't like their statistics or because they are missing a certain control group. What I think is worthy of the label ghost psychology is the kind of psychology done by people who not so much subscribe to a theory as have a mind-set with no real empirical *cash value* (to use once more a term beloved by the American Pragmatists) and that has nothing to say about the mechanisms of how we can do what we can do.

In illustration of this I will look at a position that is the opposite of my own: the view that socio-cultural processes (not innate, dedicated, biological mechanisms) carry the explanatory burden for human mentality. I'll contrast two ways of arguing for the sociocultural view: one *not* ghostly, one ghostly. In the first place we have the work of Cecilia Heyes, whom I mentioned at the start of the Cambridge section (we only overlapped for a couple of years). Her intellectual background — mind-set if you like — comprises of an interest in learning mechanisms of the kind studied in the laboratory rat, Daniel Dennett's essentially behaviouristic view of mentality (he studied under Ryle), and the evolutionary epistemology of Donald. T. Campbell. This last theory is essentially Skinnerian behaviourism as applied to the evolution of knowledge, a view that locates the growth of human knowledge in terms of the blind variation and selective retention of ideas — paralleling the way a lab-rat produces operants (actions) which the environment selects. And it's also Darwinian (random mutations selected by the environment). Think of Campbell as The Anti-Fodor. Indeed, Fodor dislikes the blind-variation-and-selective-retention models of acquisition so much he has famously turned on Darwin,[109] as mentioned earlier.

Given this, Heyes sets out to explain what we usually take to be highly socio-cognitive achievements such as imitation and theory of mind (she, in common with many others calls it "mind-reading") in terms of instrumental and associative mechanisms. They are not grounded in biological systems that exist prior to experience, and cannot be explicated except in socio-cultural terms. Also, when it comes to claims about the cognitive abilities of animals and human babies she is something of village sceptic.[110] She can, for example make a good fist of explaining imitation as a species of associative

---

[109] See: Jerry Fodor & Massimo Piattelli-Palmarini, *What Darwin Got Wrong* (New York: Farrer, Straus and Giroux, 2010). A more accessible treatment is to be found in *The London Review of Books* on 18th October, 2007 by Fodor called "Why Pigs don't have Wings."

[110] Gertrude Stein called Ezra Pound "the village explainer" going on to say this was OK if you were a village "but if not, not."

learning,[111] and she is a necessary thorn in the side of people like me who see the many demonstrations of early infant ability (in theory of mind say) as evidence for innate competence. She explains the performance in terms of low-level associative processes.[112] Moreover, she sees what she calls mind-reading as being similar to *reading*: something we learn from others, something (implicitly?) taught. She does consider neuro-cognitive preparedness of course, but only to downplay it. For example, much of the widely trumpeted mirror-neuron work,[113] she, claims, can be explained associatively.

Then on the other hand we have the work of what I'll call the "socio-lumpens." While these people may be very successful (holding professorships in good departments, being widely cited) essentially they are the heirs of the 1970s "human-sense" brigade. Their mantra was then and is now: "It's the social *con*text!" Here is an illustration: Claire Hughes (*not* a lumpen!), my ex-graduate-student and now, I'm pleased to say, one of the new colleagues I

---

[111] See Cooper, R. P., Cook, R., Dickinson, A. & Heyes, C. M. (2013) Associative (not Hebbian) learning and the mirror neuron system. *Neuroscience Letters, 540,* 28-36. And Heyes, C. M. (2011) Automatic imitation. *Psychological Bulletin,* 137, 463–483.

[112] Heyes, C. M. (2014) Rich interpretations of infant behaviour are popular but are they valid? *Developmental Science, 17,* 665-666.

[113] See footnote 111 for Heyes' work on mirror neurones. While their existence in humans is a matter of dispute, it was found in monkeys that the same pattern of neural activation is present when they (say) pick up a raisin as when they see another monkey do so. The idea being that they represent the other's action by mirroring it as their own.

actually welcome over from Free School Lane has been for a number of years doing work on the relationship between social understanding and executive functioning. This was work that grew out of our research in the early '90s on the links between theory-of-mind impairments and executive impairments in autism (p.178). More recently she has been studying so-called hard-to-manage children, who lack both social awareness and self-control. Well, this relation (executive-social) has been seized on by the lumpens as a way of explaining away the functioning of the executive system — a biological system — in terms of socio-cultural factors. They are buoyed up by research showing that Chinese children have a different executive profile from Western children. Centrally, they have what looks like a mixture of fear of and contempt for the cognitive-biological level of explanation. One of them recently referred to "boring, representational" work, meaning work on early infant capacities (what they can mentally represent), when discussing a conference paper. The lumpens are actually quite pathetic. As for the notion of "representation" (see the original discussion of this in the context of animal learning – p.39), if you don't like this concept then you don't like psychology. The lumpens should become sociologists; though I doubt the sociologists would have them.

Q. *All you are saying really is that you like and respect her and can't stand them. This is your bottom-line as ever — the <u>personal</u>.*

J.R. Not at all. I am saying that Heyes is working at the biological level — what could be more biological than Pavlovian conditioning! — and that the lumpens hate the biological level, or they fear it, to recycle a phrase of Jerry Bruner's, "like a child walking past a graveyard."

Q. *Be that as it may, what has all this got to do with ghost psychology?*

JR. I am saying — actually trying to show — that in taking "psychology" to mean something other than "the study of how we are able to do what we can do," which essentially requires the biological level, you give open house to the Teddy Smailes, the Rita Hawksmoors, the Fabian Kleins, the Kentigern Joneses, and all the rest of them. I would say Heyes is studying how we are able to do what we can do, though from a radically empiricist position and lumpens are doing something else — indulging in rhetoric.

Q. *"Something else…" What could be vaguer!*

JR. I did say in my very first paragraph that king-of the-ghosts psychology cannot be crisply defined. I also said that king-of the-ghosts psychology is best understood as a set of cases, which was part of the reason for the autobiographical narrative. And by the way, I failed to mention the lumpens' predilection for explaining children's performance on theory-of-mind tasks in terms of "narrativity" — now there's a cheesy non-postulate if there ever was one.

Q. *We are getting over-heated again. You said near the beginning that your position would turn out to look like a kind of existentialism. That seems very strange, especially in light of the Sartre-derived slogan "existence precedes essence." If you are a nativist there must be an awful lot of essence there right from the start.*

JR. It is certainly a very mild kind of existentialism. I don't buy all the stuff about "the absurd" for example. It is as mild as my "descriptive dualism" is mild. In any event, far from being at odds with my position, this mild existentialism grows directly out of what I say about our concept of mind needing to be that of a capacity-mind or mind$_c$. It is *mind$_d$* that has an *essence*. If your view of mind is mind$_c$ then it is precisely the human capacity for *free action* that is the wonder and the explicandum: the vast array of innate capacities that enable free action. At the centre of this — and this is one of the thousand reasons that trying to reduce executive functioning to something cultural is so foolish — is the capacity we have for the inhibition of "prepotent" responses (strong-but-wrong action tendencies). This idea is at least as old as the *I Ching*: "Where the moods of the heart are concerned, one should never ignore the possibility of inhibition, for this is the basis of all human freedom" (Richard Wilhelm's translation of line 3 of hexagram number 31).

In passing, I am more or less at one with Josef Perner who roots executive inhibition in our representational theory of mind — another story.[114] I am also rather keen on the idea of trying to live "authentically:" trying to take responsibility for what we did and how we are turning out.

Q.   *But surely you agree with the idea of innate dispositions. I mean within an individual. And surely that is a curb on freedom.*

JR.   Certainly not, the very idea of free action without a background of dispositions is self-defeating. How could you choose, for example, between tea and coffee if you had no particular preference? It would be like mentally tossing a coin, or just saying: "To hell with it, I'll have coffee." Imagine if, before we were born, we lined up to chose our innate dispositions. We could only do so by preferring some to others! And of course a good existentialist (and some adolescents) will tend perversely

---

[114]   Josef Perner would not put it like this, but the general idea is that if an agent is to inhibit a prepotent response then some appreciation is required of being caused to do the wrong thing — as opposed to freely intending to do it. If one lacks a conception of intention then it is difficult to see how one could have the correlative idea of being lured to do something non-intentionally. For Perner's argument: Perner, J. (1998). The meta-intentional nature of executive functions and theory of mind. In P. Carruthers & J. Boucher (Eds), *Language and thought. Cambridge, UK: Cambridge University Press.*

to do what they don't like just to show they are free. We can do that.

Q. *Yet again, I ask what all this has to do directly with your ghost psychology.*

JR. The ghost psychologists of the mind$_d$ kind are forever telling people what they are like. Where they are on O.C.E.A.N. — that they are repressed, or failing to establish a realistic life project. Need I go on? On the basis of this they give themselves a spurious authority. Talking of authority, let us turn to the greatest nativist of all, Chomsky, and the fact that he calls himself a left-anarchist. If you attribute to people a rich array of innate cognitive and moral capacities you will resist the idea that they need a ruling class to keep them in order and tell them what's what. I hope I am anti-authority in both senses — psychological and political.

Q. *And where's your so-called cash-value of all this for the practice if psychology?*

JR. I am thinking not so much of academic psychology as of the professional practitioners of "psychology." The therapists, psychodynamic and otherwise, are able to thrive as they do because their clients generally accept that this person to whom I am making out an enormous cheque knows things about the human mind that I do not.

Q.   *But you said earlier on that Freud was not on the ghost
side of the fence, because he tried to describe the
mechanisms necessary for "keeping it together" —
repression and the like. It seems to me you're just listing
the things you dislike again.*

JR.   I have never been in therapy, by the way; but I know a lot
of people who have been. I would say that Freud is one
thing and those who make a living out of psychodynamic
therapy are another. Their promiscuous ascription of
unconscious motivation, for example, is partly a matter of
an intelligence deficit. One instance: I heard of a case
where the client had trouble parking and was ten minutes
late. The therapist told her she was demonstrating an
unconscious desire not to see him. And sometimes you
hear real horror stories, especially from the further
reaches,[115] like Kleinian therapy. I have heard of
brainwashing amounting to mental torture of the
therapist's own family. They get away with it because
some people have the false belief that if you are trained in
this that or the other school you know something about
The Mind.

---

[115] Whilst revising this text, I happened to hear Elizabeth Loftus on the radio; which
spurs this late interjection. She is the experimental psychologist who first
demonstrated beyond reasonable doubt that false episodic memories can easily
be implanted in subjects by semantic cueing. What's more, she has been
foremost in drawing lessons from this work for the so-called "uncovering" of
abuse memories in psychotherapeutic clients who had never previously reported
them. For this, she has been the victim of endless, virulent abuse, and even
death threats. On 17/11/16 she was awarded the John Maddox Prize for
promoting sound science; and she is the very best of experimental psychology.

In sharp contrast there is CBT and mindfulness, which tell us what we can *do* — about our capacities for self-reflective reasoning and for calming the ruminating mind by meditation techniques.

Q.   *But surely none of this is relevant to academic psychology.*

JR.   The "Freud versus the psychodynamic flotsam" touches on what I said a little earlier. I mean, it's a matter of *how* you do something, a matter of how much intelligence you expend on doing it. Indeed of how much you have at your disposal. One can also, for example, think about the distinction between Cecilia Heyes and some of the people who emulate her, people who are simply determined to give as low-level an account of some mental capacity as possible. They just think it would be cool to, say, explain joint attention as instrumental or classical conditioning. You need to be clever to argue for wildly implausible positions!

Q.   *That last sentence brings me round to the matter of tone. You must accept that you reveal yourself as somewhat arrogant, seeming to look down, for example, on those of the PBST intake who are desperate to learn about personality. What's wrong with that!*

JR. Like me in 1966, they in 2015 confuse an interest in people in all their fascinating variety with the desire of personality theorists to categorise, to taxonomise mind$_d$. An interest in personality differences is as old as the hills. Look at the Iliad and at how Homer allows individuals to draw self-portraits simply by speaking up — the nervy, over-digressive, self-referential speech of the otherwise brave and skilful warrior Pandaros (Book 5) for instance. The infuriating Paris, the admirable Odysseus. It's *psychological* pleasure to read about them, as well as a literary one.

Q. *OK, but I sense a desire for there to be <u>less</u> psychology. You've hardly written a <u>vade mecum</u> have you...*

JR. I have to own up to that. In the late '60s young people tended to be interested in politics and sociology — the social world outside their heads. There has been a turning inward, I think. Sometimes it can take a very nasty turn, this turning inward. I've just heard about a book that's coming out by a personality theorist. He claims to show that people who are very low on Agreeableness and Conscientiousness on the dreaded O.C.E.A.N. quintet are (a) more likely to claim benefits and (b) tend to have a lot of children who they can claim for. I believe he links this to certain genes. Hey! Why not include a saliva swab when you screen the deserving from the undeserving poor.

Surely, people are either entitled to state benefits or they are not. I for one don't give a damn about whether the ones who play the system have certain personality profiles, gene-linked or not. It's the turning inward – turning away from politics, ethics, social theory, from a consideration what's actually right or wrong and what we should do. It's pretty squalid stuff. I can just imaging him saying his piece on *Start the Week* or the *Today* programme. And people seem so happy to ascribe authority to these people, as if the psychological level, rather than the moral level, were the bottom line.

And sometimes the turning away from the socio-political world and towards the mental world in which you can let your ghostly theories about people float free is just silly. My favourite recent example here of this. When the Commonwealth Games were being held in Glasgow a couple of years back, the city council had the idea of blowing up the Red Road flats as part of the opening ceremony to show the world that Glasgow was oriented towards a brave new modern future, not stuck in the past: "an unforgettable statement of how Glasgow is confidently embracing the future" the council said. The idea was abandoned, thank God. Anyway, I bet good money that some idiot psychologist had been consulted here, or somebody somewhere fancied himself as a bit of a psychologist.

Perhaps there is necessarily a problem with minds studying the mind, a problem you won't find in other sciences. And on this theme, I'll go the whole hog and finish where I began, with Wallace Stevens. Here is the beginning and ending of his poem 'Cuisine Bourgeoise'.:

> *These days of disinheritance, we feast*
> *On human heads [....*
>   *....]*   *This bitter meat*
> *Sustains us ....Who, then, are they, seated here?*
> *Is the table a mirror in which they sit and look?*
> *Are they men eating reflections of themselves?*

Q. *OK, tell me this. You keep making the point that one should have a thick membrane between the arts and the sciences, indeed between literature and psychology in particular, and yet one can hardly move in your text for poetry snippets. Even the title of the book is from a poem.*

JR. Ironic, isn't it.

INDEX

Note: The asterisks after names (e.g., Klein,* Fabian) denote masked identities.

www.ingramcontent.com/pod-product-compliance
Lightning Source LLC
Chambersburg PA
CBHW032345280326
41935CB00008B/453